The Science of Knowing

Rudolf Steiner

The Science of Knowing
Outline of an Epistemology
Implicit in the Goethean World View
With Particular Reference to Schiller

MERCURY PRESS
Spring Valley, New York

This is the first Mercury Press edition of
The Science of Knowing; it is a new translation of
*Grundlinien einer Erkenntnistheorie der Goetheschen
Weltanschauung mit besonderer Rücksicht auf Schiller
(Bibliographie No. 2)*, 7th edition GA 1979, published by the
Rudolf Steiner Nachlassverwaltung, Dornach, Switzerland.
Translation from the original German by
William Lindeman. A prior translation is available under
the title *A Theory of Knowledge*, published by the
Anthroposophic Press.

Cover design and lettering by Peter Stebbing.
Cover form by Rudolf Steiner.

Library of Congress Catalog Card Number: 88-092669
ISBN 0-936132-97-3
Copyright © 1988 by William Lindeman

Printed and published in the USA by
MERCURY PRESS
241 Hungry Hollow Road
Spring Valley, NY 10977

CONTENTS

Preface to the New Edition of 1924

This epistemology of the Goethean world view was written by me in the middle of the 1880's. Two thought-activities were living in my soul at that time. One of these was directed toward Goethe's creative work and was striving to give shape to the view of the world and of life that emerges as the moving power in this creative work. It seemed to me that something fully and purely human held sway in everything that Goethe gave the world as he created, contemplated, and lived. It seemed to me that nowhere in recent times were inner certainty, harmonious completeness, and a sense for reality with respect to the world as fully represented as in Goethe. From this thought arose the recognition that the way Goethe conducted himself in the activity of knowing is also the one that emerges from the essential being of man and of the world.

On the other hand, my thoughts were living within the philosophical views prevalent at that time regarding the essential being of knowledge. In these views the activity of knowing was threatening to encapsulate itself within the being of man himself. Otto Liebmann, the gifted philosopher, had made the statement that human consciousness cannot reach beyond itself. It must remain within itself. Whatever, as true reality, lies beyond the world that consciousness shapes within itself, of this it can know nothing. In brilliant writings Otto Liebmann elaborated this thought in relation to the most varied areas of man's world of experience. Johannes Volkelt had written his thoughtful books *Kant's Epistemology* and *Experience and Thinking*. In the world given to man he saw only a complex of mental pictures that arise through man's relationship to a world which in itself is unknown. He did, in fact, concede that within the experience of thinking a necessity manifests itself when thinking reaches into the world of mental pictures. In a certain way one feels as if one were bursting through the world of mental pictures into reality when thinking becomes active. But what has been gained by this? One could thereby feel justified in forming judgments in thinking that say something about the real world; but with such judgments one still stands entirely within the inner life of man; nothing of the essential being of the world penetrates into him.

In epistemological questions, Eduard von Hartmann, whose philosophy was of real use to me even though I could not accept its basic premises or conclusions, took exactly the same standpoint that Volkelt then presented in detail.

It was everywhere acknowledged that the human being, in his activity of knowing, strikes up against certain limits through which he cannot penetrate into the realm of true reality.

Confronting all this there stood for me the fact—inwardly experienced, and known in the experiencing—that man with his thinking, if he deepens it sufficiently, does live in the midst of world reality as within a spiritual reality. I believed I possessed this knowledge as one that can stand in human consciousness with the same inner clarity as that which manifests in mathematical knowledge.

In the face of this knowledge the opinion cannot persist that there are limits of knowledge *such* as those believed to have been established by the trend of thought just described.

Into all this there played the fact that my thoughts were drawn to the theory of evolution, which was then in full bloom. In Haeckel it had assumed a form that did not allow the self-sustained being and working of the spiritual to be taken into account. The later, the more perfect, was supposed to have emerged in the course of time out of the earlier, the less developed. I could see that this was so insofar as outer, sense-perceptible reality was concerned. Nevertheless, I was too familiar with the self-sustaining spirituality that is not dependent upon the sense-perceptible and is established within itself to admit that the outer, sense-perceptible world of phenomena was right in this regard. Rather, it was a matter of building a bridge from this world of the senses to that of the spirit. In the course of time, as thought of in terms of sense perceptions, the human spiritual seems to evolve out of the preceding unspiritual.

Yet the sense-perceptible, rightly known, shows everywhere that it is a manifestation of the spiritual. In the face of this correct knowledge of the sense-perceptible, it was clear to me that "limits of knowledge," as they were then set, could be acknowledged only by someone who encounters this sense-perceptible realm and then treats it in the way a person would treat a printed page if he simply looked at the forms of the letters, and, knowing nothing about reading, then declared that one cannot know what lies behind these forms.

In this way my attention was drawn to the path from sense observation to the spiritual, which for me was a fact established through inner, knowing experience. I was not seeking unspiritual atomic worlds behind sense-perceptible phenomena; I sought the spiritual, which seemingly manifests within the inner life of the human being but which in actuality belongs to the things and processes of the sense world themselves. Because of the way man carries out his knowing activity, it might *seem* as though the thoughts of things were within man, whereas in actuality they hold sway within the things. It is necessary for man, in this experiencing of what *seems* to be the case, to separate the thoughts of things from the things; in the true experience of knowledge, he gives them back again to the things.

The evolution of the world is then to be understood in such a way that the preceding unspiritual, out of which the spirituality of man later unfolds itself, contains something spiritual above and beyond itself. The later, spiritualized sense-perceptibility in which man appears thus arises through the fact that the spirit ancestor of man unites himself with the imperfect, unspiritual forms, and, transforming these, then appears in sense-perceptible form.

These trains of thought led me beyond the epistemologists of that time, whose acumen and scientific sense of responsibility I fully acknowledged. They led me to Goethe.

I can well recall today my inner struggles back then. I did not make it easy for myself to break away from the philosophical trains of thought prevalent at that time. But my guiding star was always the recognition, brought about entirely through itself, of the fact that the human being can behold himself inwardly as a spirit independent of the body, standing in a purely spiritual world.

Before my works on Goethe's natural-scientific writings and before this epistemology, I wrote a little essay on atomism that has never been published. It took the direction I just indicated. I must recall the happiness it gave me when Friedrich Theodor Vischer, to whom I sent the essay, responded with a few favorable comments.

But now, from my studies of Goethe, it became clear to me how my thoughts led me to behold the essential being of knowledge that emerges everywhere in Goethe's creative activity and in his stance toward the world. I found that my viewpoints provided me with an epistemology that is the epistemology of the Goethean world view.

4

In the 1880's I was recommended by Karl Julius Schröer, my teacher and fatherly friend to whom I owe a great deal, to write the introductions* to Goethe's natural-scientific writings for Kürschner's *National Literatur* and to tend to the publishing of these writings. In the course of this work I pursued Goethe's cognitive life in all the areas in which he was active. It became increasingly clear to me, right down into the details, that my own view brought me into the epistemology implicit in the Goethean world view. And so I wrote this present epistemology during my work on Goethe's natural-scientific writings.

As I look at it again today, it also appears to me to be the epistemological foundation and justification for everything I said and published later. It speaks of the essential being of knowing activity that opens the way from the sense-perceptible world into the spiritual one.

It might seem strange that this work of my youth, almost forty years old now, should appear today unchanged and expanded only by some notes. In its manner of presentation it bears the earmarks of a thinking that lived in the philosophy of forty years ago. If I were writing it today, I would state many things differently. But I would not be able to present anything different as the essential being of knowledge. Yet what I would write today would not be able to bear within itself so faithfully the *germ* of the world view for which I have stood and which is in accordance with the spirit. One can write in such a germinal way only at the beginning of a life of knowledge. This perhaps justifies a new publication of a youthful work in this unchanged form. The epistemologies that existed at the time of its writing have found their continuation in later ones. I said what I

* These introductions are now published in book form under the title *Goethean Science*, Mercury Press, 1988—Ed.

have to say about them in my book *The Riddles of Philosophy.* This book is appearing now in a new edition from the same publisher.

What I sketched years ago in this little book as the epistemology implicit in the Goethean world view seems to me just as necessary to say today as it was forty years ago.

Goetheanum in Dornach
November, 1923
Rudolf Steiner

Foreword to the First Edition

When Professor Kürschner honored me with the task of publishing Goethe's natural-scientific works for *German National Literature*, I was well aware of the difficulties confronting me in such an undertaking. I had to work against a view that had become almost universally established. While the conviction is becoming more and more widespread that Goethe's *literary works* are the foundation of our entire cultural life, his scientific efforts are regarded—even by those who go the farthest in their appreciation of them—as nothing more than *inklings* he had of truths that then became fully validated in the course of scientific investigation. The eye of his genius, they say, attained inklings of natural lawfulnesses which then, *independently* of him, were rediscovered by the strict methods of science. What one fully grants to the rest of Goethe's activity—namely, that every educated person must come to terms with it—is denied him with respect to his scientific view. It is not acknowledged at all that the poet's scientific works afford anything that science, even without him, would not offer today.

By the time I was introduced to Goethe's world view by K.J. Schröer, my beloved teacher, my thinking had already taken a direction that enabled me to look beyond the poet's individual discoveries to the essential point: to the way Goethe fit each individual discovery into the totality of his conception of nature, to the way he evaluated it in order to gain insight into the relationship of nature beings, or, as he so aptly expressed it himself (in the essay *Power to Judge in Beholding**), in order to participate spiritually in nature's productions. I soon recognized that the achievements

* *Anschauende Urteilskraft*

7

which modern science does grant Goethe are the inessential ones, whereas precisely what is significant is overlooked. The individual discoveries would really have been made even without Goethe's research; but science will be deprived of his marvelous conception of nature as long as it does not draw this directly from him. This realization gave the direction that had to be taken by the introductions to my edition of Goethe's scientific works. They had to show that every single view expressed by Goethe is to be traced back to the totality of his genius.

The principles by which this is to be done are the subject of this little book. It undertakes to show that what we set forth as Goethe's scientific views is also capable of being established on its own independent foundation.

This seems to me to be sufficient introduction to the following study. There remains only the pleasant duty of expressing my most deeply felt thanks to Professor Kürschner, who has lent me his friendly assistance with this little book with the same extraordinary kindness he has always shown my scientific endeavors.

End of April, 1886
Rudolf Steiner

A. PRELIMINARY QUESTIONS

1. The Point of Departure

When we trace any one of the major streams of present-day spiritual life back to its sources, we always encounter one of the spirits of our classical period. Goethe or Schiller, Herder or Lessing has given an impulse, and from it one or another spiritual movement has taken its start and still continues on today. Our whole German cultural life is so fully based on our classical writers that many a person who thinks himself completely original actually manages nothing more than to express what Goethe or Schiller indicated long ago. We have lived so fully into the world they created that hardly anyone who leaves the path they indicated could expect our understanding. Our way of *looking at* the world and at life is so influenced by them that no one can rouse our interest who does not seek points of reference with this world.

There is only *one* branch of our spiritual-cultural life that, we must admit, has not yet found any such point of reference. It is that branch of science which goes beyond merely collecting observations, beyond information about individual phenomena, in order to provide a satisfying overview of the world and of life. It is what one usually calls philosophy. For philosophy, our classical period does not seem to exist at all. It seeks its salvation in an artificial seclusion and noble isolation from the rest of spiritual life. This statement is not refuted by the fact that a considerable number of older and more recent philosophers and natural scientists have occupied themselves with Goethe and Schiller. For they have not arrived at their scientific standpoint by bringing to fruition the seeds contained in the scientific achievements of those heroes of the spirit. They arrived at their scientific standpoint *outside* of the world view put forward by Schiller and Goethe and then *afterwards* compared the two. They did not make this comparison for the purpose of *gaining* something for their own cause from the scientific views of the classical thinkers, but rather in order to test these thinkers to see how they stood up in the light of their own cause. We will come back to this in more detail. But first we would like just to indicate the consequences for this realm of science that arise out of the stance it takes toward the highest level of cultural development in modern times.

A great number of educated readers today will immediately reject unread any literary or scientific book that appears with a claim to being philosophical. There has hardly ever been a time when philosophy has enjoyed less favor than now. Leaving aside the writings of Schopenhauer and Eduard von Hartmann, which take up questions concerning life and the world, questions of the most general interest, and which therefore have been widely read, one does not go too far in saying that philosophical works are read today only by people in the profession. Nobody bothers except them. An educated person not in the profession has the vague feeling: This literature[1]* contains nothing that meets my spiritual needs; the things dealt with there do not concern me; they are not connected in any way with what is necessary for the satisfaction of my spirit. Only the fact we have indicated can bear the guilt for this lack of interest in all philosophy, for, in contrast to this lack of interest, there stands an ever-growing need for a satisfying view of the world and of life. What for a long time was a substitute for so many people, i.e., religious dogma, is losing more and more of its power to convince. The urge is increasing all the time to achieve by the work of *thinking* what

* See Notes to the New Edition, p. 121—Ed.

10

was once owed to *faith in revelation: satisfaction of spirit*. The involvement of educated people could therefore not fail to exist if the sphere of science about which we are speaking really went hand in hand with the whole development of culture, if its representatives took a stand on the big questions that move humanity.

One must always keep one's eye on the fact that it can never be a question of first creating artificially a spiritual need, but only of seeking out the need that exists and satisfying it. The task of science* is not to pose questions[2] but rather to consider questions carefully when they are raised by human nature and by the particular level of culture, and then to *answer* them. Our modern philosophers set themselves tasks that are in no way a natural outgrowth of the level of culture at which we stand; therefore no one is asking for their findings. But this science passes over the questions that our culture *must pose* by virtue of the vantage point to which our classical writers have raised it. *We therefore have a science [present-day philosophy] that no one is seeking, and a scientific need that is not being satisfied by anyone.*

Our central science—the science that should solve the actual riddles of the world for us—cannot be an exception among all the other branches of spiritual life. It must seek its sources where they have found theirs. It must not just come to terms with our classical thinkers; it must also seek in them the seeds for its own development; the same impulse must sweep through it as through the rest of our culture. This necessity resides in the very nature of the matter. It is also due to this necessity that modern researchers have occupied themselves with the classical writers in the way al-

---

* *Wissenschaft*: "science" in the broader sense, from *scire*, to know.— Ed.

ready described above. But this shows nothing more than that one had a vague feeling of the impermissibility of passing over the convictions of these thinkers and simply proceeding with the order of the day. But this also shows that one did not really manage to develop *their* views any further. The way one approached Lessing, Herder, Goethe, and Schiller shows this. Despite all the excellence of many of the books about these thinkers, one must still say, regarding almost everything written about Goethe's and Schiller's scientific* works, that it did not develop organically out of their views but was rather brought afterwards into relationship to them. Nothing demonstrates this better than the fact that the most contrary scientific theories have regarded Goethe as the thinker who had earlier "inklings" of their views. World views having absolutely nothing in common with each other point to Goethe with seemingly equal justification when they feel the need to see their standpoints recognized as being at the height of human development. One cannot imagine a sharper antithesis than between the teachings of Hegel and Schopenhauer. The latter calls Hegel a charlatan and his philosophy vapid word-rubbish, pure nonsense, barbaric word-combinations. These two men actually have absolutely nothing in common with each other except an unlimited reverence for Goethe and the belief that he adhered to their world view.

And it is no different with more recent scientific theories. Haeckel, who has elaborated Darwinism brilliantly and with iron consistency, and whom we must regard as by far the most significant follower of the English scientist, sees his own view prefigured in the Goethean one. Another natural scientist of the present day, C.F.W. Jessen, writes

* Again: "scientific" in the broader sense—Ed.

of Darwin's theory: "The stir caused among many specialists and laymen by this theory—which had often been set forth earlier and just as often refuted by thorough research, but which is now propped up by many seeming supports—shows, unfortunately, how little people know and understand the results of natural-scientific research." The same researcher says of Goethe that he "rose to comprehensive investigations into inorganic as well as organic nature" by finding, "through intelligent, deeply penetrating contemplation of nature, the basic law of all plant formation." Each of these researchers can bring, in utterly overwhelming numbers, proofs of the agreement of his scientific theory with the "intelligent observations of Goethe." It would put the unity of Goethe's thought in a very dubious light if both of these standpoints could justifiably cite it as their authority. The reason for this phenomenon, however, lies precisely in the fact that not one of these views, after all, has really grown out of the Goethean world view, but rather each has its roots outside it. The reason lies in the fact that one seeks an *outer* agreement of one's view with details torn out of the wholeness of Goethe's thinking, which thereby lose their meaning; one does not want to attribute to this wholeness itself the *inner worthiness* to found a scientific direction. Goethe's views were never the *starting point* of scientific investigations but always only an *object of comparison.* Those who concerned themselves with him were rarely *students*, devoting themselves to his ideas without preconceptions, but rather *critics*, sitting in judgment over him.

One says, in fact, that Goethe had far too little scientific sense; the worse a philosopher, the better a poet he was. Therefore it would be impossible to base a scientific standpoint on him. This is a total misconception about

13

Goethe's nature. To be sure, Goethe was no *philosopher* in the usual sense of the word; but it should not be forgotten that the wonderful harmony of his personality led Schiller to say: "The poet is the only *true human being.*" What Schiller understood here by "true human being" was Goethe. There was not lacking in his personality any element that belongs to the highest expression of the universally human. But all these elements united in him into a totality that works *as such*. *This* is how it comes about that a *deep philosophical sense* underlies his views about nature, even though this philosophical sense does not come to consciousness in him in the form of definite scientific principles. Anyone who enters more deeply into that totality will be able, if he also brings along a philosophical disposition, to separate out that philosophical sense and to present it as Goethean science. But he must take his start from Goethe and not approach him with an already fixed view. Goethe's spiritual powers always work in a way that accords with the strictest philosophy, even though he did not leave behind any systematic presentation of them.

Goethe's world view* is the most many-sided imaginable. It issues from a center resting within the unified nature of the poet, and it always turns outward the side corresponding to the nature of the object being considered. The unity of the spiritual forces being exercised lies in Goethe's nature; the *way* these forces are exercised at any given moment is determined by the object under consideration. Goethe takes his way of looking at things from the outer world and does not force any particular way upon it. These days, however, the thinking of many people is active in only *one* particular way; it is useful for only one category of objects; it is not, like that of Goethe, *unified* but rather

* See also Rudolf Steiner's *Goethe's World View*, Mercury Press, 1985.

uniform. Let us express this even more precisely: There are people whose intellect is especially able to think purely mechanical interdependencies and effects; they picture the whole universe as a mechanism. Other people have an urge to perceive everywhere the mysterious mystical element in the outer world; they become adherents of mysticism. All error arises when a way of thinking like this which *is* valid for one category of objects is declared to be universal. In this way the conflict between the many world views is explained. If such a one-sided conception approaches the Goethean one, which is not limited—because it does not in any way take its way of looking at things from the spirit of the beholder but rather from the nature of what is beheld— then it is comprehensible that the one-sided conception fastens onto those elements of thought in the Goethean conception that are in accord with itself. Goethe's world view encompasses many directions of thought in the sense just indicated and cannot, in fact, ever be imbued with any single, one-sided conception.

The philosophical sense that is an essential element in the organism of Goethe's genius has significance also for his literary works. Even though it was far from Goethe's way to present in a conceptually clear form what this sense communicated to him, as Schiller could, it was nevertheless still a factor contributing to his artistic work, as it was with Schiller. The literary productions of Goethe and Schiller are unthinkable without the world view that stands in the background. With Schiller this is expressed more in the basic principles he actually formulated, with Goethe more in the *way he looked at things.* Yet the fact that the greatest poets of our nation, at the height of their creative work, could not do without that philosophical element proves more than anything else that this element is a necessary part of the history of humanity's development. Precisely this dependence on Goethe and Schiller will make it possible to wrest our central science [philosophy] out of its academic isolation and to incorporate it into the rest of cultural development. The scientific convictions of our classical writers are connected by a thousand threads to their other strivings and are of a sort *demanded* by the cultural epoch that created them.

2. The Science of Goethe According to the Method of Schiller

With the foregoing we have determined the direction the following investigations will take. They are meant to develop what manifested in Goethe as a scientific sense and to interpret his way of looking at the world.

The objection could be made that this is not the way to present a view scientifically. Under no circumstances should a scientific view be based on an authority; it must always rest upon principles. Let us forestall this objection at once. We regard a view founded in the Goethean world conception as *true*, not because it can be traced back to this world conception, but because we believe that we can support the Goethean world view upon sound, basic principles and present it as one well founded in itself. The fact that we take Goethe as our starting point should not prevent us from being just as serious about *establishing* the views we present as are the proponents of any science supposedly free of all presuppositions. *We are presenting the Goethean world view, but we will establish it in accordance with the demands of science.*

Schiller has already indicated the direction of the path such investigations must take. No one perceived the great-

16

ness of Goethe's genius more clearly than he did. In his letters to Goethe, Schiller held up to him a mirror image of Goethe's being; in his letters *On the Aesthetic Education of Man*, he traces his ideal of the artist back to the way he recognized it in Goethe; and in his essay *On Naive and Sentimental Poetry*, he portrays the being of true art in the form in which he found it in Goethe's poetry. At the same time, this justifies the statement that our considerations are built on the foundation of Goethe's and Schiller's world view. We wish to look at Goethe's scientific thinking by that method for which Schiller provided the model. Goethe's gaze is directed upon nature and upon life, and his way of looking at things in doing so will be the *object* (the content) of our discussion; Schiller's gaze is directed upon Goethe's spirit, and *his* way of looking at things in doing so will be the ideal for our *method*.

In this way we believe Goethe's and Schiller's scientific strivings are made fruitful for the present day.

In accordance with current scientific terminology, our work must be considered to be *epistemology*. To be sure, the questions with which it deals will in many ways be of a different nature from those usually raised by this science. We have seen why this is the case. Wherever similar investigations arise today, they take their start almost entirely from Kant. In scientific circles the fact has been completely overlooked that in addition to the science of knowledge founded by the great thinker of Königsberg, there is yet another direction, at least potentially, that is no less capable than the Kantian one of being deepened in an objective manner. In the early 1860's Otto Liebmann made the statement that we must go back to Kant if we wish to arrive at a world view free of contradiction. This is why today we have a literature on Kant almost too vast to encompass.

But this Kantian path will not help the science of philosophy. Philosophy will play a part in cultural life again only when, instead of going back to Kant, it immerses itself in the scientific conception of Goethe and Schiller.

And now let us approach the basic questions of a science of knowledge corresponding to these introductory remarks.

3. The Task of Science

Ultimately it is true for all science what Goethe expressed so aptly with the words: "In and for itself, theory* is worth nothing, except insofar as it makes us believe in the interconnections of phenomena." Through science we are always bringing separate facts of our experience into a connection with each other. In inorganic nature we see causes and effects as separate from each other, and we seek their connections in the appropriate sciences. In the organic world we perceive species and genera of organisms and try to determine their mutual relationships. In history we are confronted with the individual cultural epochs of humanity; we try to recognize the inner dependency of one stage of development upon the other. Thus each science has to work within a particular domain of phenomena in the sense of the Goethean principle articulated above.

Each science has its own area in which it seeks the interconnections of phenomena. But there still remains a great polarity in our scientific efforts: between the ideal** world achieved by the sciences on the one hand and the objects that underlie it on the other. There must be a science that also elucidates the interrelationships here. The ideal and

---

* *Theorie.* In German, this word still connotes more of the sense of the Greek original: what thinking "sees."—Ed.

**Throughout this book, "ideal" usually means "in the form of ideas."—Ed.

the real world, the polarity of idea and reality, these are the subject of such a science. These opposites must also be known in their interrelationship.

To seek these relationships is the purpose of the following discussion. The existence of science on the one hand, and nature and history on the other are to be brought into a relationship. What significance is there in the mirroring of the outer world in human consciousness; what connection exists between our thinking about the objects of reality and these objects themselves?

B. EXPERIENCE

4. Determining the Concept of Experience

Two regions confront each other therefore: our thinking, and the objects with which thinking concerns itself. To the extent that these objects are accessible to our observation, one calls them the content of experience *(Erfahrung)*. For the moment let us leave aside entirely the question as to whether, outside our field of observation, there are yet other objects of thinking and what their nature might be. Our immediate task will be to define sharply the boundaries of the two regions indicated: experience and thinking. We must first have experience in its particular delineation before us and then investigate the nature of thinking. Let us proceed with the first task.

What is experience? Everyone is conscious of the fact that his thinking is kindled in conflict with reality. The objects in space and in time approach us; we perceive a highly diversified outer world of manifold parts, and we experience a more or less richly developed inner world. The first form in which all this confronts us stands finished before us. We play no part in its coming about. Reality at first presents itself to our sensible and spiritual grasp as though springing from some beyond unknown to us. To begin with we can only let our gaze sweep across the manifoldness confronting us.

This first activity of ours is grasping reality with our senses. We must hold onto what it thus presents us. For only this can be called pure experience.[3]

We feel the need right away to penetrate with organizing intellect the endless manifoldness of shapes, forces, colors, sounds, etc., that arises before us. We try to become clear about the mutual interdependencies of all the single entities confronting us. If we encounter an animal in a certain region, we ask about the influence of this region upon the life of the animal; if we see a stone begin to roll, we seek the other events with which this is connected. But what results from such asking and seeking is no longer *pure experience*. It already has a twofold origin: experience and thinking.

Pure experience is the form of reality in which reality appears to us when we confront it to the complete exclusion of what we ourselves bring to it.

The words Goethe used in his essay *Nature*[4] are applicable to this form of reality: "We are surrounded and embraced by her. She takes us up, unasked and unwarned, into the orbit of her dance."

With objects of the external sense world, this leaps so obviously to the eye that scarcely anyone would deny it. A body confronts us at first as a multiplicity of forms, colors, warmth and light impressions, which are suddenly before us as though sprung from some primal source unknown to us.

The conviction in psychology that the sense world, as it lies before us, is nothing in itself but is only a product of the interworking of an unknown molecular outer world with our organism does not contradict our statement. Even if it were really true that color, warmth, etc., were nothing more than the way our organism is affected by the outer world, still the process that transforms the happening of the outer world into color, warmth, etc., lies entirely outside *consciousness*. No matter what role our organism may play in this, it is not molecular processes that lie before our thinking as the finished form in which reality presses in upon us (experience); rather it is those colors, sounds, etc.

The matter is not so clear with respect to our inner life. But closer consideration will banish all doubt here about

21

the fact that our inner states also appear on the horizon of our consciousness in the same form as the things and facts of the outer world. A feeling presses in upon me in the same way that an impression of light does. The fact that I bring it into closer connection with my own personality is of no consequence in this regard. We must go still further. Even thinking itself appears to us at first as an object of experience. Already in approaching our thinking investigatively, we set it before us; we picture its first form to ourselves as coming from something unknown to us.

This cannot be otherwise. Our thinking, especially if one looks at the form it takes as individual activity within our consciousness, is *contemplation*; i.e., it directs its gaze outward upon something that is before it. In this it remains at first mere activity. It would gaze into emptiness, into nothingness, if something did not confront it.

Everything that is to become the object of our knowing must accommodate itself to this form of confrontation. We are incapable of lifting ourselves above this form. If, in thinking, we are to gain a means of penetrating more deeply into the world, then thinking itself must first become experience. *We must seek thinking among the facts of experience as just such a fact itself.*

Only in this way will our world view have inner unity. It would lack this unity at once if we wanted to introduce a foreign element into it. We confront experience pure and simple and seek within *it* the element that sheds light upon itself and upon the rest of reality.

5. An Indication as to the Content of Experience

Let us now take a look at pure experience. What does it contain, as it sweeps across our consciousness, without our working upon it in thinking? It is mere juxtaposition in space and succession in time; an aggregate of utterly disconnected particulars. None of the objects that come and go there has anything to do with any other. At this stage, the facts that we perceive, that we experience inwardly, are of no consequence to each other.

This world is a manifoldness of things of equal value. No thing or event can claim to play a greater role in the functioning of the world than any other part of the world of experience. If it is to become clear to us that this or that fact has greater significance than another one, we must then not merely observe the things, but must already bring them into thought-relationships. The rudimentary organ of an animal, which perhaps does not have the least importance for its organic functioning, is for *experience* of exactly the same value as the most essential organ of the animal's body. This greater or lesser importance will in fact become clear to us only when we begin to *reflect* upon the relationships of the individual parts of observation, that is, when we work upon experience.

For *experience*, the snail, which stands at a low level of organization, is the equal of the most highly developed animal. The difference in the perfection of organization appears to us only when we grasp the given manifoldness conceptually and work it through. The culture of the Eskimo, in this respect, is also equal to that of the educated European; Caesar's significance for the historical development of humanity appears to *mere experience* as being no greater than that of one of his soldiers. In the history of literature, Goethe does not stand out above Gottsched, if it is a matter of merely experienceable factuality.

At this level of contemplation, the world is a completely smooth surface for us with respect to thought. No part of this surface rises above another; none manifests any kind

23

of conceptual difference from another. It is only when the spark of thought strikes into this surface that heights and depths appear, that one thing appears to stand out more or less than another, that everything takes form in a definite way, that threads weave from one configuration to another, that everything becomes a harmony complete within itself.

We believe that these examples suffice to show what we mean by the greater or lesser significance of the objects of perception (here considered to be synonymous with the things of experience), and what we mean by that knowing activity which first arises when we contemplate these objects in their *interconnection*. At the same time, we believe that in this we are safe from the objection that our world of experience in fact shows endless differences in its objects even *before* thinking approaches it. After all, a red surface differs from a green one even if we do not exercise any thinking. This is correct. If someone wanted to refute us by this, however, he would have misunderstood our argument totally. This is precisely our argument, that an endless number of *particulars* is what experience offers us. These particulars must of course differ from one another; otherwise they would not in fact confront us as an endless, disconnected manifoldness. It is not at all a question of perceived things being undifferentiated, but rather of their complete unrelatedness, and of the absolute insignificance of the individual sense-perceptible facts for the *totality* of our picture of reality. It is precisely because we recognize this endless qualitative differentiation that we are driven to our conclusions.

If we were confronted by a self-contained, harmoniously organized unity, we could not then say, in fact, that the individual parts of this unity are of no significance to one another.

24

If, for this reason, someone does not find the comparison we used above to be apt, he has not grasped it at the actual point of comparison. It would be incorrect, of course, for us to want to compare the world of perception, in all its infinitely diverse configuration, to the uniform regularity of a plane. But our plane is definitely not meant to represent the diverse world of phenomena, but rather the *homogeneous total picture* we have of this world as long as thinking has not approached it. After the activation of our thinking, each particular of this total picture no longer appears in the way our senses alone communicate it, but already with the significance it has for *the whole* of reality. It appears then with characteristics totally lacking to it in the form of experience.

In our estimation, Johannes Volkelt has succeeded admirably in sketching the clear outlines of what we are justified in calling pure experience. He already gave a fine characterization of it five years ago in his book on *Kant's Epistemology*, and has then carried the subject further in his most recent work, *Experience and Thinking*. Now he did this, to be sure, in support of a view that is utterly different from our own, and for an essentially different purpose than ours is at the moment. But this need not prevent us from introducing here his excellent characterization of pure experience. He presents us, simply, with the pictures which, in a limited period of time, pass before our consciousness in a completely unconnected way. Volkelt says: "Now, for example, my consciousness has as its content the mental picture of having worked hard today; immediately joining itself to this is the content of a mental picture of being able, with good conscience, to take a walk; but suddenly there appears the perceptual picture of the door opening and of the mailman entering; the mailman appears, now sticking

25

out his hand, now opening his mouth, now doing the reverse; at the same time, there join in with this content of perception of the mouth opening, all kinds of auditory impressions, among which comes the impression that it is starting to rain outside. The mailman disappears from my consciousness, and the mental pictures that now arise have as their content the sequence: picking up scissors, opening the letter, criticism of illegible writing, visible images of the most diverse written figures, diverse imaginings and thoughts connected with them; scarcely is this sequence at an end than again there appears the mental picture of having worked hard and the perception, accompanied by ill humor, of the rain continuing; but both disappear from my consciousness, and there arises a mental picture with the content that a difficulty believed to have been resolved in the course of today's work was not resolved; entering at the same time are the mental pictures: freedom of will, empirical necessity, responsibility, value of virtue, absolute chance, incomprehensibility, etc.; these all join together with each other in the most varied and complicated way; and so it continues."

Here we have depicted, within a certain limited period of time, what we really *experience*, the form of reality in which *thinking* plays no part at all.

Now one definitely should not believe that one would have arrived at a different result if, instead of this everyday experience, one had depicted, say, the experience we have of a scientific experiment or of a particular phenomenon of nature. Here, as there, it is individual unconnected pictures that pass before our consciousness. Thinking first establishes the connections.

We must also recognize the service rendered by Dr. Richard Wahle's little book, *Brain and Consciousness*

(Vienna, 1884), in showing us in clear contours what is actually given by experience divested of everything of a thought-nature, with only one reservation: that what Wahle presents as the characteristics applying absolutely to the phenomena of the outer and inner world actually applies only to the *first stage* of the world contemplation we have characterized. According to Wahle we know only a juxtaposition in space and a succession in time. For him there can be absolutely no question of a relationship between the things that exist in this juxtaposition and succession. For example, there may after all be an inner connection somewhere between the warm rays of the sun and the warming up of a stone; but we know nothing of any causal connection; all that becomes clear to us is that a second fact follows upon the first. There may also be somewhere, in a world inaccessible to us, an inner connection between our brain mechanism and our spiritual activity; we only know that both are events running their courses parallel to each other; we are absolutely not justified, for example, in assuming a causal connection between these two phenomena.

Of course, when Wahle also presents this assertion as an ultimate truth of science, we must dispute this broader application; his assertion is completely valid, however, with respect to the first *form* in which we become aware of reality.

It is not only the things of the outer world and the processes of the inner world that stand there, at this stage of our knowing, without interconnection; our own personality is also an isolated entity with respect to the rest of the world. We find ourselves as *one* of innumerable perceptions without connection to the objects that surround us.

6. Correcting an Erroneous Conception of Experience as a Whole

At this point we must indicate a preconception, existing since Kant, which has already taken root so strongly in certain circles that it is considered axiomatic. If anyone were to question it, he would be described as a dilettante, as one who has not risen above the most elementary concepts of modern science. The preconception I mean is the view: It is already established from the very beginning that the whole world of perception, this endless manifoldness of colors and shapes, of sounds and warmth differentiations, etc., is nothing more than our subjective world of mental pictures *(Vorstellungen)*, which exists only as long as we keep our senses open to what works in upon them from a world unknown to us. This view declares the entire world of phenomena to be a mental picture *inside* our individual consciousness, and on the foundation of this presupposition one then erects further assertions about the nature of our activity of knowing. Even Volkelt adhered to this view and founded upon it his epistemology, which is masterful with respect to its scientific execution. Even so, this preconception is not a *fundamental truth* and is in no way qualified to stand at the *forefront* of the science of knowledge.

But do not misunderstand us. We do not wish to raise what would certainly be a vain protest against the *physiological* achievements of the present day. But what is entirely justified physiologically is still far from being qualified on that basis to be placed at the portals of epistemology. One may consider it to be an irrefutable physiological truth that only through the participation of our organism does the complex of sensations and perceptions arise that we have called experience. But the fact remains, nevertheless, that any such knowledge can only be the result of many considerations and investigations. This characterization—that our phenomenal world, in a *physiological sense*, is of a subjective nature—is already what thinking *determines* it to be, and has therefore absolutely nothing to do with the initial appearance of this world. This characterization already presupposes that *thinking* has been applied to *experience*. The examination of the relationship between these two factors of knowing activity must therefore precede this characterization.

By this view, people believed themselves elevated above the pre-Kantian "naïveté" that regarded things in space and time as reality, just as the naive person with no scientific education still does today.

Volkelt asserts "that all acts claiming to be an objective activity of knowing are inextricably bound to the knowing individual consciousness; that all such acts occur immediately and directly only within the consciousness of the individual; and that they are utterly incapable of reaching beyond the sphere of the individual person and of grasping or entering the sphere of reality lying outside it."

It is nevertheless still the case that an unprejudiced thinking could never discover what it is about the form of reality which approaches us directly (experience) that could in any way justify us in characterizing it as mere mental picture.

This simple reflection—that the naive person notices absolutely nothing about things that could bring him to this view—shows us that in the objects themselves there lies *no* compelling reason for this assumption. What is there about a tree or a table itself that could lead me to regard it as a mere configuration of mental pictures? At the very least this cannot therefore be presented as an obvious truth.

By presenting it as an obvious truth, Volkelt entangles himself in a contradiction with his own basic principles. In our view, he had to be untrue to the truth acknowledged by him—that experience contains nothing but an unconnected chaos of pictures without any conceptual characterization—in order to be able to assert the subjective nature of that same experience. Otherwise, he would have had to see that the subject of knowing activity, the contemplator, stands just as unrelated within the world of experience as any other object in it. But if one applies to the perceived world the predicate *"subjective,"* this is just as much a *conceptual characterization* as when one regards a falling stone as the *cause* of the depression in the ground. But Volkelt himself, after all, does not wish to acknowledge any connection whatsoever between the things of experience. Therein lies the contradiction in his view; this is where he became untrue to the principle he stated with respect to pure experience. By doing this he encloses himself within his individuality and is no longer capable of emerging from it. Indeed, he admits this without reservation. Everything remains doubtful to him that lies beyond the disconnected pictures of our perceptions. In his view, our thinking does indeed struggle to draw inferences from this world of mental pictures about an objective reality; it is just that going beyond this world cannot lead to really sure truths. According to Volkelt all knowing that we attain through thinking is not protected from doubt. In terms of certainty it cannot compare at all with direct experience. Only direct experience can provide a knowing not to be doubted. But we have seen how defective this knowing is.

But all this indeed stems only from the fact that Volkelt applies to sense-perceptible reality (experience) a characteristic that cannot pertain to it in any way, and then he builds up his further assumptions on this presupposition.

We had to pay particular attention to Volkelt's book because it is the most significant contemporary achievement in this sphere, and also because it can be taken as the prototype for all the epistemological efforts which, in principle, stand in opposition to the direction we are presenting on the basis of the Goethean world view.

7. Calling upon the Experience of Every Single Reader

We wish to avoid the error of attributing any characteristic beforehand to the directly "given," to the first form in which the outer and inner world appear, and of thus presenting our argument on the basis of any *presupposition.* In fact, we are characterizing experience as precisely that in which our thinking plays no part at all. There can be no question, therefore, of any error in thinking at the beginning of our argument.

The basic error of many scientific endeavors, especially those of the present day, consists precisely of the fact that they believe they present pure experience, whereas in fact they only gather up the concepts again that they themselves have inserted into it. Someone could object that we have also assigned a whole number of attributes to pure experience. We called it an endless manifoldness, an aggregate of unconnected particulars, etc. Are those then not conceptual characterizations also? In the sense in which we use them, certainly not. We have only made use of these concepts in order to direct the reader's eye to reality free of thoughts. We do not wish to ascribe these concepts to experience; we make use of them only in order to direct at-

31

tention to that form of reality which is devoid of any concept.

All scientific investigations must, in fact, be conducted in the medium of language, and it can only express concepts. But there is, after all, an essential difference between using certain words in order to attribute this or that characteristic directly to a thing, and making use of words only in order to direct the attention of the reader or listener to an object. To use a comparison, we could say: It is one thing for A to say to B, "Observe that man in the circle of his family and you will gain a very different impression of him than if you get to know him only through the way he is at work"; it is another if A says, "That man is an excellent father." In the first case, B's attention is directed in a certain sense; he is called upon to judge a personality under certain circumstances. In the second case a particular characteristic is simply ascribed to this personality; an assertion is therefore made. Just as the first case relates to the second, so we believe the starting point of our book relates to the starting point of other books on this subject. If, because of necessities of style or possibilities of expression, the matter appears at any point to be other than this, let us state here expressly that our discussions have only the intention just described and are far from any claim to having asserted anything pertaining to the things themselves.

If we now wished to have a name for the first form in which we observe reality, we believe that the expression that fits the matter the very best is: *manifestation to the senses.*[5] By *sense* we do not mean merely the outer senses, the mediators of the outer world, but rather *all* bodily and spiritual organs whatsoever that serve the perception of immediate facts. It is, indeed, quite usual in psychology to use the expression *inner sense* for the ability to perceive inner experiences.

Let us use the word *manifestation*, however, simply to designate a thing perceptible to us or a perceptible process insofar as these appear in space or in time.

We must still raise a question here that is to lead us to the second factor we have to consider with respect to a science of knowledge: to *thinking*.

Must we regard the form of experience we have described thus far as how things actually are? Is it a characteristic of reality? A very great deal depends upon answering this question. If this form of experience *is* an essential characteristic of the things of experience, if it is something which, in the truest sense of the word, belongs to them by their very nature, then one could not imagine how one is ever to transcend this stage of knowing at all. One would then simply have to resort to writing down everything we perceive, in disconnected notes, and our science would be a collection of such notes. For what would be the purpose of any investigation into the interconnection of things if the complete isolation we ascribe to them in the form of experience were truly characteristic of them?

The situation would be entirely different[6] if, in this form of reality, we had to do not with reality's essential being but only with its inessential outer aspect, if we had only the shell of the true being of the world before us which hides this being and challenges us to search further for it. We would then have to strive to penetrate this shell. We would have to take our start from this first form of the world in order then to possess ourselves of its true (essential) characteristics. We would then have to overcome its *manifestation to the senses* in order to develop out of it a higher form of manifestation.—The answer to this question is given in the following investigations.

C. THINKING

8. Thinking as a Higher Experience within Experience

We find, within the unconnected chaos of experience, and indeed at first also as a fact of experience, an element that leads us out of unconnectedness. It is *thinking*. Even as a fact of experience within experience, thinking occupies an exceptional position.

With the rest of the world of experience, if I stay with what lies immediately before my senses, I cannot get beyond the particulars. Assume that I have a liquid which I bring to a boil. At first it is still; then I see bubbles rise; the liquid comes into movement and finally passes over into vapor form. Those are the successive individual perceptions. I can twist and turn the matter however I want: if I remain with what the senses provide, I find no connection between the facts. With thinking this is not the case. If, for example, I grasp the thought "cause," this leads me by its own content to that of "effect." I need only hold onto the thoughts in the form in which they appear in direct experience and they manifest already as lawful characterizations.

What, for the rest of experience, must first be brought from somewhere else—if it is applicable to experience at all—namely, *lawful interconnection*, is already present in thinking in its very first appearance. With the rest of experience the whole thing does not already express itself in what appears as manifestation to my consciousness; with thinking, the whole thing arises without reservation in what is given me. With the rest of experience I must penetrate the shell in order to arrive at the kernel; with thinking, shell and kernel are one undivided unity. It is only due to a general human limitation that thinking appears to us at first

35

as entirely analogous to the rest of experience. With thinking we merely have to overcome *our own* limitation. With the rest of experience we must solve a difficulty lying in *the thing* itself.

In thinking, what we must seek for with the rest of experience has itself become direct experience.

With this the solution is given to a difficulty that will hardly be solved in any other way. That we stick to experience is a justified demand of science. But no less so is the demand that we seek out the inner lawfulness of experience. *This inner being itself must therefore appear at some place in experience as experience.* In this way experience is deepened with the help of experience itself. Our epistemology imposes the demand for experience in its highest form; it rejects any attempt to bring something into experience from outside it. Our epistemology finds, within experience, even the characterizations that thinking makes. The way in which thinking enters into manifestation is the same as with the rest of the world of experience.

The principle of experience, in its implications and actual significance, is usually misunderstood. In its most basic form it is the demand that we leave the objects of reality in the first form in which they appear and only in this way make them objects of science. This is a purely methodological principle. It expresses absolutely nothing about the content of what is experienced. If someone wanted to assert, as materialism does, that only the *perceptions of the senses* can be the object of science, then he could *not* base himself on this principle. This principle does not pass any judgment as to whether the content is sense-perceptible or ideal. But if, in a particular case, this principle is to be applicable in the most basic form just mentioned, then, to be sure, it makes a presupposition. For, it demands that the objects, as they are experienced, already have a form that suffices for scientific endeavor. With respect to the experience of the outer senses, as we have seen, this is not the case. This occurs only with respect to thinking.

Only with respect to thinking can the principle of experience be applied in its most extreme sense.

This does not preclude our extending the principle of experience also over the rest of the world. It has in fact other forms besides its most extreme one. If, for the purpose of scientific explanation, we cannot leave an object in the form in which it is directly perceived, this explanation can nevertheless still occur in such a way that the means it requires are brought in from other regions of the world of experience. In doing so we still have not stepped outside the region of *"experience in general."*

A science of knowledge established in the sense of the Goethean world view lays its chief emphasis on the fact that it remains absolutely true to the principle of experience. No one recognized better than Goethe the total validity of this principle. He adhered to the principle altogether as strictly as we demanded earlier. All higher views on nature had to appear to him in no form other than as experience. They had to be "higher nature within nature."

In his essay "Nature," Goethe says that we are incapable of getting outside nature. If we therefore wish to explain nature to ourselves in his sense, we must find the means of doing so *within* nature.

But how could one found a science of knowing upon the principle of experience if in experience itself we did not find at any point the basic element of what is scientific: ideal* lawfulness? We need only take up this element, as we have

* i.e., "in the form of ideas."—Ed.

seen; we need only delve into this element. For, it is to be found within experience.

Now, does thinking really approach us in such a way, does our individuality become conscious of it in such a way, that we are fully justified in claiming for it the characteristics stressed above? Anyone who directs his attention to this point will find that there is an essential difference between the way an outer manifestation of sense-perceptible reality becomes conscious—yes, even the way any other process of our spiritual life becomes conscious—and the way we become aware of our own thinking. In the first case we are definitely conscious of confronting a finished thing; finished, namely, insofar as it has come into manifestation without our having exercised upon this becoming any *determining* influence. It is different with respect to thinking. It is only at first glance that thinking seems to be like the rest of experience. When we grasp any thought, we know, by the total immediacy with which it enters our consciousness, that we are most inwardly connected with the way it arises. Even when a thought occurs to me quite suddenly, whose appearance therefore seems in a certain sense entirely like that of an outer event which my eyes and ears must first mediate for me, I nevertheless know that the field upon which this thought comes to manifestation is *my* consciousness; I know that *my* activity must first be called upon in order for the sudden thought to come about. With every outer object, I am sure that the object at first turns only its outer aspect toward my senses; with a thought, I clearly know that what the thought turns toward me is at the same time its *all*, that it enters my consciousness as a totality complete in itself. The outer driving forces that we must always presuppose with sense-perceptible objects are not present with a thought. Indeed it is to those outer forces that we must ascribe the fact that sense phenomena confront us as something finished; we must credit these outer forces with the *becoming* of phenomena. With a thought, it is clear to me that its *becoming* is not possible without my activity. I must work the thought through, must recreate its content, must experience it inwardly right into its smallest parts if it is to have any significance for me at all.

Thus far we have arrived at the following truths. At the first stage of our contemplation of the world, the whole of reality confronts us as an unconnected aggregate; thinking is included within this chaos. If we move about within this manifoldness, we find one part in it which, already in the form of its first appearance, has the character the other parts have yet to acquire. This part is thinking. What is to be overcome in the rest of experience, namely the form of its immediate appearance, is precisely what we must hold onto with thinking. Within our consciousness we find this factor of reality, our thinking, that is to be left in its original form, and we are bound up with it to such an extent *that the activity of our spirit is at the same time the manifesting of this factor.* It is one and the same thing, looked at from two sides. This thing is the thought-content of the world. On the one hand it manifests as an *activity of our consciousness,* on the other as *a direct manifestation of a lawfulness complete in itself, as a self-determined ideal content.* We will see right away which aspect has the greater importance.

Now, because we stand *inside* this thought-content, because we permeate it in all its component parts, we are capable of really knowing its *most essential nature.* The way it approaches us is a guarantee of the fact that the characteristics we earlier ascribed to it really are its due. Therefore it can definitely serve as a starting point for every further kind of contemplation of the world. From this *thought-content itself* we can conclude what its *essential* character is; but if we wish to determine the essential character of anything else, we must begin our investigations with this thought-content. Let us articulate this still more clearly. *Since we experience a real lawfulness, an ideal definement, only in thinking, the lawfulness of the rest of the world, which we do not experience from this world itself, must also lie already contained in thinking.* In other words: *manifestation to the senses* and *thinking* stand over against each other in experience. The first, however, gives us no enlightenment about its own essential being; the latter gives us enlightenment both about *itself* and about the essential being of the *manifestation to the senses*.

9. Thinking and Consciousness

Now, however, it seems as though we ourselves are bringing in the subjective element here, which we had wanted so decisively to keep out of our epistemology. Although the rest of the perceptual world does not bear a subjective character—as one could gather from our discussions— thoughts do, in fact, bear such a character, even according to our view.

This objection is based on a confusion of two things: the stage upon which our thoughts appear, and the element which determines their content, from which they receive their inner lawfulness. We definitely do not produce a thought-content as though, in this production, we were the ones who determined into which connections our thoughts are to enter. We only provide the opportunity for the thought-content to unfold itself *in accordance with its own nature.* We grasp thought *a* and thought *b* and give them the opportunity to enter into a lawful connection by bringing them into mutual interaction with each other. It is not

40

our subjective organization that *determines* this particular connection between *a* and *b* in precisely one particular way and no other. *The human spirit effects the joining of thought-masses only in accordance with their content.* In thinking we therefore fulfill the principle of experience in its most basic form.

This refutes the view of Kant, of Schopenhauer, and in a broader sense also of Fichte, which states that the laws we assume for the purpose of explaining the world are only a result of our own spiritual organization and that we *lay* them into the world only by virtue of our spiritual individuality.

One could raise yet another objection from the subjectivistic standpoint. Even if the lawful connection of thought-masses is not brought about by us in accordance with our organization but rather is dependent upon their content, still, this very content itself might be a purely subjective product, a mere quality of our spirit; thus we would only be uniting elements that we ourselves first created. Then our thought-world would be no less a subjective semblance. It is very easy to meet this objection, however. If it had any basis, we would then be connecting the content of our thinking according to laws whose origins would truly be unknown to us. If these laws do not spring from our subjectivity—and this subjectivity is the view we disputed earlier and can now regard as refuted—then what should provide us with laws by which to interconnect a content we ourselves create?

Our thought-world is therefore an entity fully founded upon itself; it is a self-contained totality, perfect and complete in itself. Here we see which of the two aspects of the thought-world is the essential one: the *objective* aspect of its content, and *not* the *subjective* aspect of the way it arises.

This insight into the inner soundness and completeness of thinking appears most clearly in the scientific system of Hegel. No one has credited thinking, to the degree he did, with a power so complete that it could found a world view out of itself. Hegel had an *absolute trust* in thinking; it is, in fact, the only factor of reality that he trusted in the true sense of the word. But no matter how correct his view is in general, he is still precisely the one who totally discredited thinking through the all too extreme form in which he defended it. The way he presented his view is to blame for the hopeless confusion that has entered our "thinking about thinking." He wanted to make the significance of thoughts, of ideas, really visible by declaring the necessity in thought to be at the same time the necessity in the factual world. He therefore gave rise to the error that the characterizations made by thinking are not purely ideal ones but rather factual ones. One soon took his view to mean that he sought, in the world of sense-perceptible reality, even thoughts as though they were objects. He never really did make this very clear. *It must indeed be recognized that the field of thoughts is human consciousness alone.* Then it must be shown that the thought-world forfeits none of its objectivity through this fact. Hegel demonstrated only the objective side of thoughts, but most people see only the subjective side, because this is easier; and it seems to them that he treated something purely ideal as though it were an object, that he made it into something mystical. Even many contemporary scholars cannot be said to be free of this error. They condemn Hegel for a failing he himself did not have, but which, to be sure, one can impute to him because he did not clarify this matter sufficiently.

We acknowledge that there is a difficulty here for our power of judgment. But we believe that this difficulty can be overcome by energetic thinking. We must picture two things to ourselves: first, that we *actively* bring the ideal world into manifestation, and at the same time, that what we actively call into existence *is founded upon its own laws.* Now admittedly, we are used to picturing a phenomenon in such a way that we need only approach it and passively observe it. This is not an absolute requirement, however. No matter how unusual it might be for us to picture that we ourselves actively bring something objective into manifestation—that we do not merely perceive a phenomenon, in other words, but produce it at the same time—it is not inadmissible for us to do so.

One simply needs to give up the usual opinion that there are as many thought-worlds as there are human individuals. This opinion is in any case nothing more than an old preconception from the past. It is tacitly assumed everywhere, without people realizing that there is another view at least just as possible, and that the reasons must first be weighed as to the validity of one or the other. Instead of *this* opinion, let us consider the following one: There is absolutely only *one single* thought-content, and our individual thinking is nothing more than our self, our individual personality, working its way into the *thought-center* of the world. This is not the place to investigate whether this view is correct or not, but it is *possible*, and we have accomplished what we wanted; we have shown that what we have presented as the necessary objectivity of thinking can easily be seen not to contradict itself even in another context.

With regard to objectivity, the work of the thinker can very well be compared with that of the mechanic. Just as the mechanic brings the forces of nature into mutual interplay and thereby effects a purposeful activity and release of power, so the thinker lets the thought-masses enter into lively interaction, and they develop into the thought-systems that comprise our sciences.

Nothing sheds more light on a view than exposing the errors that stand in its way. Let us call upon this method once again as one that has often been used by us to advantage.

One usually believes that we join certain concepts into larger complexes, or that we think in general in a certain way, because we feel a certain inner (logical) compulsion to do so. Even Volkelt adheres to this view. But how does this view accord with the *transparent clarity* with which our entire thought-world is present in our consciousness? We know absolutely nothing in the world more exactly than our thoughts. Now can it really be supposed that a certain connection is established on the basis of an inner *compulsion*, where everything is so clear? Why do I need the compulsion, if I know the nature of what is to be joined, know it through and through, and can therefore guide myself by *it*? All our thought-operations are processes that occur on the basis of *insight* into the entities of thoughts and not according to a compulsion. Any such compulsion contradicts the nature of thinking.

Nonetheless, it could be the case that it is the nature of thinking to impress its content into its own manifestation at the same time, and that, because of our spirit's organization, we are nevertheless unable to perceive this content directly. But this is not the case. The way thought-content approaches us is our guarantee that here we have before us the essential being of the thing. We are indeed conscious of the fact that *we* accompany every process in the thought-world with our spirit. One can nevertheless think of the form of manifestation only as being determined by the *essential being of the thing*. How would we be able to *reproduce* the form of manifestation if we did not know the essential being of the thing? One can very well think that the form of manifestation confronts us as a finished totality and that we *then* seek its core. But one absolutely cannot believe that one is a co-worker in this *production* of the phenomenon without effecting this production from within the core.

10. The Inner Nature of Thinking

Let us take another step toward thinking. Until this point we have merely looked at the position thinking takes toward the rest of the world of experience. We have arrived at the view that it holds a very privileged position within this world, that it plays a *central role*. Let us disregard that now. Let us limit ourselves here to the *inner* nature of thinking. Let us investigate the thought-world's very own character, in order to experience how *one* thought depends upon the *other* and how the thoughts relate *to each other*. Only by this means will we first be able to gain enlightenment about the question: What is *knowing activity*? Or, in other words: What does it mean to make thoughts for oneself about reality; what does it mean to want to come to terms with the world through thinking?

We must keep ourselves free of any preconceived notions. It would be just such a preconception, however, if we were to presuppose that the concept (thought) is a picture, *within* our consciousness, by which we gain enlightenment about an object lying outside our consciousness. We are not concerned here with this and similar presuppositions. We take thoughts as we find them. Whether they have a relationship to something else or other, and what this relationship might be, is precisely what we want to investigate. We should not therefore place these questions here

45

as a starting point. Precisely the view indicated, about the relationship of concept and object, is a very common one. One often defines the concept, in fact, as the spiritual image of things, providing us with a faithful photograph of them. When one speaks of thinking, one often thinks only of this presupposed relationship. One scarcely ever seeks to travel through the realm of thoughts, for once, within its own region, in order to see what one might find there.

Let us investigate this realm as though there were nothing else at all outside its boundaries, as though thinking were *all of reality*. For a time we will disregard all the rest of the world.

The fact that one has failed to do this in the epistemological studies basing themselves on Kant has been disastrous for science. This failure has given a thrust to this science in a direction utterly antithetical to our own. By its whole nature, this trend in science can never understand Goethe. It is in the truest sense of the word *un-Goethean* for a person to take his start from a doctrine that he does not find in observation but that he himself inserts into what is observed. This occurs, however, if one places at the forefront of science the view that between thinking and reality, between idea and world, there exists the relationship just indicated. One acts as Goethe would only if one enters deeply into thinking's own nature itself and then observes the relationship that results when this thinking, known in *its* own being, is then brought into connection with experience.

Goethe everywhere takes the route of experience in the strictest sense. He first of all takes the objects as they are and seeks, while keeping all subjective opinions completely at a distance, to penetrate their nature; he then sets up the conditions under which the objects can enter into mutual interaction and waits to see what will result. Goethe seeks to give nature the opportunity, in particularly characteristic situations that he establishes, to bring its lawfulness into play, to express its laws itself, as it were.

How does our thinking manifest to us when looked at for itself? It is a *multiplicity* of thoughts woven together and organically connected in the most manifold ways. But when we have sufficiently penetrated this multiplicity from all directions, it simply constitutes a unity again, a harmony. All its parts relate to each other, are there for each other; one part modifies the other, restricts it, and so on. As soon as our spirit pictures two *corresponding* thoughts to itself, it notices at once that they actually flow together into one. Everywhere in our spirit's thought-realm it finds elements that belong together; *this* concept joins itself to *that one*, a third one elucidates or supports a fourth, and so on. Thus, for example, we find in our consciousness the thought-content "organism"; when we scan our world of mental pictures, we hit upon a second thought-content: "lawful development, growth." It becomes clear to us at once that both these thought-contents belong together, that they merely represent two sides of one and the same thing. But this is how it is with our whole system of thoughts. All individual thoughts are parts of a great whole that we call our world of concepts.

If any *single* thought appears in my consciousness, I am not satisfied until it has been brought into harmony with the rest of my thinking. A separate concept like this, set off from the rest of my spiritual world, is altogether unbearable to me. I am indeed conscious of the fact that there exists an inwardly established harmony between all thoughts, that the world of thoughts is a unified one. Therefore every such isolation is unnatural, untrue.

If we have struggled through to where our whole thought-world bears a character of complete inner harmony, then through it the contentment our spirit demands becomes ours. *Then we feel ourselves to be in possession of the truth.*

As a result of our seeing *truth* to be the thorough-going harmony of all the concepts we have at our command, the question forces itself upon us: Yes, but does thinking even have any content if you disregard all visible reality, if you disregard the sense-perceptible world of phenomena? Does there not remain a total void, a pure phantasm, if we think away all sense-perceptible content?

That this is indeed the case could very well be a widespread opinion, so we must look at it a little more closely. As we have already noted above, many people think of the entire system of concepts as in fact only a photograph of the outer world. They do indeed hold onto the fact that our knowing develops in the *form* of thinking, but demand nevertheless that a "strictly objective science" take its content only from outside. According to them the outer world must provide the substance that flows into our concepts. Without the outer world, they maintain, these concepts are only empty schemata without any content. If this outer world fell away, concepts and ideas would no longer have any meaning, for they are there for the sake of the outer world. One could call this view the negation of the concept. For then the concept no longer has any significance at all for the objective world. It is something *added onto* the latter. The world would stand there in all its completeness even if there were no concepts. For they in fact bring nothing new to the world. They contain nothing that would not be there without them. They are there only because the knowing subject wants to make use of them in order to have, in a form appropriate to this subject, that which is otherwise already there. For this subject, they are only mediators of a content that is of a *non-conceptual* nature. This is the view presented.

If it were justified, one of the following three presuppositions would have to be correct.

1. The world of concepts stands in a relationship to the outer world such that it only reproduces the entire content of this world in a different form. Here "outer world" means the sense world. If that were the case, one truly could not see why it would be necessary to lift oneself above the sense world at all. The entire whys and wherefores of knowing would after all already be given along with the sense world.

2. The world of concepts takes up, as its content, only a part of "what manifests to the senses." Picture the matter something like this. We make a series of observations. We meet there with the most varied objects. In doing so we notice that certain characteristics we discover in an object have already been observed by us before. Our eye scans a series of objects A, B, C, D, etc. A has the characteristics p, q, a, r; $B: l, m, b, n$; $C: k, h, c, g$; and $D: p, u, a, v$. In D we again meet the characteristics a and p, which we have already encountered in A. We designate these characteristics as *essential*. And insofar as A and D have the same essential characteristics, we say that they are of the same kind. Thus we bring A and D together by holding fast to their essential characteristics in thinking. There we have a thinking that does not entirely coincide with the sense world, a thinking that therefore cannot be accused of being superfluous as in the case of the first presupposition above; nevertheless it it still just as far from bringing anything new to the sense world. But one can certainly raise the objection to this that, in order to recognize which characteristics

49

of a thing are *essential*, there must already be a certain *norm* making it possible to distinguish the essential from the inessential. This norm cannot lie in the object, for the object in fact contains both what is essential and inessential in undivided unity. Therefore this norm must after all be thinking's very own content.

This objection, however, does not yet entirely overturn this view. One can say, namely, that it is an unjustified assumption to declare that this or that is more essential or less essential for a thing. We are also not concerned about this. It is merely a matter of our encountering certain characteristics that are the same in several things and of our then *stating* that these things are of the same kind. It is not at all a question of whether these characteristics, which are the same, are also essential. But this view presupposes something that absolutely does not fit the facts. *Two things of the same kind really have nothing at all in common if a person remains only with sense experience.* An example will make this clear. The simplest example is the best, because it is the most surveyable. Let us look at the following two triangles.

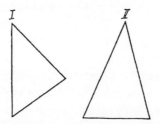

What is really the same about them if we remain with sense experience? Nothing at all. What they have in common—namely, the law by which they are formed and which

50

brings it about that both fall under the concept "triangle"—
we can gain only when we go beyond sense experience. The
concept "triangle" comprises all triangles. We do not arrive at it merely by looking at all the individual triangles.
This concept always remains the same for me no matter how
often I might picture it, whereas I will hardly ever view the
same "triangle" twice. What makes an individual triangle
into "this" particular one and no other has nothing whatsoever to do with the concept. A particular triangle is *this*
particular one not through the fact that it corresponds to
that concept but rather because of elements lying entirely
outside the concept: the length of its sides, size of its angles,
position, etc. But it is after all entirely inadmissible to maintain that the content of the *concept* "triangle" is drawn from
the objective sense world, when one sees that its content is
not contained at all in any sense-perceptible phenomenon.

3. Now there is yet a third possibility. The concept could
in fact be the mediator for grasping entities that are not
sense-perceptible but that still have a self-sustaining
character. This latter would then be the *non-conceptual
content of the conceptual form* of our thinking. Anyone who
assumes such entities, existing beyond experience, and
credits us with the possibility of knowing about them must
then also necessarily see the concept as the interpreter of
this knowing.

We will demonstrate the inadequacy of this view more
specifically later. Here we want only to note that it does
not in any case speak *against* the fact that the world of concepts has content. For, if the objects about which one
thinks lie beyond any experience and beyond thinking, then
thinking would all the more have to have within itself the
content upon which it finds its support. It could not, after

all, think about objects for which no trace is to be found within the world of thoughts.

It is in any case clear, therefore, that thinking is not an empty vessel; rather, taken purely for itself, it is full of content; and its content does not coincide with that of any other form of manifestation.

D. SCIENCE

11. Thinking and Perception

Science permeates perceived reality with the concepts grasped and worked through by our thinking. Through what our spirit, by its activity, has raised out of the darkness of mere potentiality into the light of reality, science complements and deepens what has been taken up passively. This presupposes that perception needs to be complemented by the spirit, that it is not at all something definitive, ultimate, complete.

The fundamental error of modern science is that it regards sense perceptions as something already complete and finished. It therefore sets itself the task of simply photographing this existence complete in itself. To be sure, only positivism, which simply rejects any possibility of going beyond perception, is consistent in this regard. Still, one sees in nearly all sciences today the striving to regard this as the correct standpoint. In the true sense of the word this requirement would be satisfied only by a science that simply enumerates and describes things as they exist side by side in space, and events as they succeed each other in time. The old style of natural history still comes closest to meeting this requirement. Modern natural science really demands the same thing, setting up a complete theory of experience in order then to violate it right away when taking the first step in real science.

We would have to renounce our thinking entirely if we wanted to keep to pure experience. One disparages thinking if one takes away from it the possibility of perceiving in itself entities inaccessible to the senses. In addition to sense qualities there must be yet another factor within reality that is grasped by thinking. Thinking is an organ of the human being that is called upon to observe something higher than what the senses offer. *The side of reality accessible to thinking is one about which a mere sense being would never experience anything.* Thinking is not there to rehash the sense-perceptible but rather to penetrate what is hidden to the senses. Sense perception provides only *one* side of reality. The *other* side is a thinking apprehension of the world. Now thinking confronts us at first as something altogether foreign to perception. The perception forces itself in upon us from outside; thinking works itself up out of our inner being. The content of this thinking appears to us as an organism inwardly complete in itself; everything is in strictest interconnection. The individual parts of the thought-system determine each other; every single concept ultimately has its roots in the wholeness of our edifice of thoughts.

At first glance it seems as though the inner consistency of thinking, its self-sufficiency, would make any transition to perception impossible. If the statements of thinking were such that one could fulfill them in only *one* way, then thinking would really be isolated in itself; we would not be able to escape from it. But this is not the case. The statements of thinking are such that they can be fulfilled in *manifold* ways. It is just that the element causing this manifoldness cannot itself then be sought *within* thinking. If we take one of the statements made by thought, namely that the earth attracts all bodies, we notice at once that the thought leaves open the possibility of being fulfilled in the most varied ways. But these are variations that can no longer be reached by thinking. This is the place for another element. This element is sense perception. Perception affords a kind of specialization of the statements made by thoughts, a possibility left open by these statements themselves.

It is in this specialization that the world confronts us when we merely make use of experience. Psychologically that element comes first which in point of fact is derivative.

In all cognitive treatment of reality the process is as follows. We approach the concrete perception. It stands before us as a riddle. Within us the urge makes itself felt to investigate the actual *what,* the *essential being,* of the perception, which this perception itself does not express. This urge is nothing else than a concept working its way up out of the darkness of our consciousness. We then hold fast to this concept while sense perception goes along parallel with this thought-process. The mute perception suddenly speaks a language comprehensible to us; we recognize that the concept we have grasped is what we sought as the essential being of the perception.

What has taken place here is a judgment *(Urteil).* It is different from the form of judgment that joins two concepts without taking perception into account at all. When I say that inner freedom is the self-determination of a being, from out of itself, I have also made a judgment. The parts of this judgment are concepts, which have not been given to me in perception. The inner unity of our thinking, which we dealt with in the previous chapter, rests upon judgments such as these.

The judgment under consideration here has a perception as its subject and a concept as its predicate. The particular animal in front of me is a dog. In this kind of judgment, a perception is inserted into my thought-system at a particular place. Let us call such a judgment a *perception-judgment.*

Through a perception-judgment, one recognizes that a particular sense-perceptible object, in accordance with its being, coincides with a particular concept.

If we therefore wish to grasp what we perceive, the perception must be *prefigured* in us as a definite concept. We would go right by an object for which this is not the case without its being comprehensible to us.

The best proof that this is so is provided by the fact that people who lead a richer spiritual life also penetrate more deeply into the world of experience than do others for whom this is not the case. Much that passes over the latter kind of person without leaving a trace makes a deep impression upon the former. ("Were not the eye of sunlike nature, the sun it never could behold." Goethe) Yes, someone will say, but don't we meet infinitely many things in life about which previously we had not had the slightest concept, and do we not then, right on the spot, at once form concepts of them? Certainly. But is the sum total of all possible concepts identical with the sum total of those I have formed in my life up to now? Is my system of concepts not capable of development? Can I not, in the face of a reality that is incomprehensible to me, at once bring my thinking into action so that in fact it also develops, right on the spot, the concept I need to hold up to an object? The only ability useful to me is one that allows a definite concept to emerge from the thought-world's supply. The point is not that a particular thought has already become conscious for me in the course of my life, but rather that this thought allows itself to be drawn from the world of thoughts accessible to me. It is indeed of no consequence to its content where and when I grasp it. In fact, I draw all the characterizations of thoughts out of the world of thoughts. Nothing whatsoever, in fact, flows into this content from the sense object. I only recognize *again*, within the sense object, the thought I drew up from within my inner being. This object does in fact move me at a particular moment to bring forth precisely this thought-content out of the unity of all possible thoughts, but it does not in any way provide me with the building stones for these thoughts. These I must draw out of myself.

Only when we allow our thinking to work does reality first acquire true characterization. Reality, which before was mute, now speaks a clear language.

Our thinking is the translator that interprets for us the gestures of experience.

We are so used to seeing the world of concepts as empty and without content, and so used to contrasting perception with it as something full of content and altogether definite, that it will be difficult to establish for the world of concepts the position it deserves in the true scheme of things. We miss the fact entirely that mere looking is the emptiest thing imaginable, and that only from thinking does it first receive any content at all. The only thing true about the above view is that looking does hold the ever-fluid thought in one particular form, without our having to work along actively with this holding. The fact that a person with a rich soul life sees a thousand things that are a blank to someone spiritually poor proves, clear as day, that the *content* of reality is only the mirror-image of the content of our spirit and that we receive only the empty form from outside. We must, to be sure, have the strength in us to recognize ourselves as the begetters *(Erzeuger)* of this content; otherwise we see only the mirror image and never our spirit, that is mirrored. Even a person who sees himself in a real mirror must in fact know himself as a personality in order *to know himself again* in this image.

All sense perception dissolves ultimately, as far as its essential being is concerned, into ideal content. Only then does it appear to us as transparent and clear. The sciences for the most part have not even been touched by any awareness of this truth. One considers the characterizations given by thought to be *attributes* of objects, like color, odor, etc. One therefore believes the following characterization to be a feature of all bodies: that they remain in the state of motion or rest in which they find themselves until an external influence alters this state. It is in this form that the law of inertia figures in physics. But the true state of affairs is completely different. The thought, "body," exists in my system of concepts in many modifications. One of these is the thought of a thing which, out of itself, can bring itself to rest or into motion; another is the concept of a body that alters its state only as a result of an external influence. I designate the latter kind as inorganic. If, then, a particular body confronts me that reflects back to me in the perception this second conceptual characterization, then I designate it as *inorganic* and connect with it all the characterizations that follow from the concept of an inorganic body.

The conviction should permeate all the sciences that their content is purely thought-content and that they stand in no other connection to perception than that they see, in the object of perception, a particular form of the concept.

12. Intellect and Reason

Our thinking has a twofold task: firstly, to create concepts with sharply delineated contours; secondly, to bring together the individual concepts thus created into a unified whole. In the first case we are dealing with the activity that makes distinctions; in the second, with the activity that joins. These two spiritual tendencies by no means enjoy the same cultivation in the sciences. The keen intellect that enters into the smallest details in making its distinctions is given to a significantly larger number of people than the uniting power of thinking that penetrates into the depths of beings.

For a long time one saw the only task of science to be the making of exact distinctions between things. We need only recall the state of affairs in which Goethe found natural history. Through Linnaeus it had become the ideal to seek the exact differences between individual plants in order in this way to be able to use the most insignificant characteristics to set up new species and subspecies. Two kinds of animals or plants that differed in only the most inessential things were assigned right away to different species. If an unexpected deviation from the arbitrarily established character of the species was found in one or another creature that until then had been assigned to one or another species, one did not then reflect how such a deviation could be explained from this character itself; one simply set up a new species.

Making distinctions like this is the task of the intellect *(Verstand)*. It has only to separate concepts and maintain them in this separation. This is a necessary preliminary stage of any higher scientific work. Above all, in fact, we need firmly established, clearly delineated concepts before we can seek their harmony. But we must not remain in this separation. For the intellect, things are separated that humanity has an essential need to see in a harmonious unity. Remaining separate for the intellect are: cause and effect, mechanism and organism, freedom and necessity, idea and reality, spirit and nature, and so on. All these distinctions are introduced by the intellect. They must be introduced, because otherwise the world would appear to us as a blurred, obscure chaos that would form a unity only *because it would be totally undefined for us*.

The intellect itself is in no position to go beyond this separation. It holds firmly to the separated parts.

To go beyond this is the task of reason *(Vernunft)*. It has to allow the concepts created by the intellect to pass over into one another. It has to show that what the intellect keeps strictly separated is actually an inner unity. The separation is something brought about artificially, a necessary intermediary stage for our activity of knowing, not its conclusion. A person who grasps reality in a merely intellectual way distances himself from it. He sets in *reality's* place—since it *is in truth a unity*—an artificial multiplicity, a manifoldness that has nothing to do with the *essential being* of reality.

The conflict that has arisen between an intellectually motivated science and the human heart stems from this. Many people whose thinking is not yet developed enough for them to arrive at a unified world view grasped in full conceptual clarity are, nevertheless, very well able to penetrate into the inner harmony of the universe with their feeling. Their hearts give them what reason offers the scientifically developed person.

When such people meet the intellectual view of the world, they reject with scorn the infinite multiplicity and cling to the unity that they do not know, indeed, but that they feel more or less intensely. They see very well that the intellect withdraws from nature, that it loses sight of the spiritual bond joining the parts of reality.

Reason leads back to reality again. The unity of all existence, which before was *felt* or of which one even had only dim *inklings*, is clearly penetrated and seen by reason. The intellectual view must be deepened by the view of reason. If the former is regarded as an end in itself instead of as a necessary intermediary stage, then it does not yield reality but rather a distorted image of it.

There are sometimes difficulties in connecting the thoughts that the intellect has created. The history of science provides us with many proofs of this. We often see the human spirit struggle to bridge the differences created by the intellect.

In reason's view of the world the human being merges with the world in undivided unity.

Kant pointed already to the difference between intellect and reason. He designated reason as the ability to perceive ideas; the intellect, on the other hand, is limited merely to beholding the world in its dividedness, in its separateness.

Now reason is, in fact, the ability to perceive ideas. Here we must determine the difference between concept and idea, to which we have hitherto paid no attention. For our purposes until now it has only been a matter of finding those qualities of the element of thought that present themselves in concept *and* idea. The concept is the single thought as it is grasped and held by the intellect. If I bring a number of such single thoughts into living flux in such a way that they pass over into one another, connect with one another, then thought-configurations arise that are present only for reason, that the intellect cannot attain. For reason, the creations of the intellect give up their separate existences and live on only as part of a totality. These configurations that reason has created shall be called *ideas*.

The fact that the idea leads a multiplicity of the concepts created by the intellect back to a unity was also expressed by Kant. But he presented the configurations that come to manifestation through reason as mere deceptive images, as illusions that the human spirit eternally conjures up because it is eternally striving to find some unity to experience that is never to be found. According to Kant, the unities created in ideas do not rest upon objective circumstances; they do not flow from the things themselves; rather they are merely subjective norms by which we bring order into our knowing. Kant therefore does not characterize ideas as constitutive principles, which would have to be essential to the things, but rather as regulative principles, which have meaning and significance only for the systematics of our knowing.

If one looks at the way in which ideas come about, however, this view immediately proves erroneous. It is indeed correct that subjective reason has the need for unity. But this need is without any content; it is an empty *striving* for unity. If something confronts it that is absolutely lacking in any unified nature, it cannot itself produce this unity out of itself. If, on the other hand, a multiplicity confronts it that allows itself to be led back into an inner harmony, it then brings about this harmony. The world of concepts created by the intellect is just such a multiplicity.

Reason does not presuppose any particular unity but rather the empty form of unification; reason is the ability to bring harmony to light when harmony lies within the object itself. Within reason, the concepts themselves combine into ideas. *Reason brings into view the higher unity of the intellect's concepts, a unity that the intellect certainly has in its configurations but is unable to see.* The fact that this is overlooked is the basis of many misunderstandings about the application of reason in the sciences.

To a small degree every science, even at its starting point—yes, even our everyday thinking—needs reason. If, in the judgment that every body has weight, we join the subject-concept with the predicate-concept, there already lies in this a uniting of two concepts and therefore the simplest activity of reason.

The unity that reason takes as its object is certain *before* all thinking, before any use of reason; but it is hidden, is present only as potential, does not manifest as a fact in its own right. Then the human spirit brings about separation, in order, by uniting the separate parts through reason, to see fully into reality.

Whoever does not presuppose this must either regard all connecting of thoughts as an arbitrary activity of the subjective spirit, or he must assume that the unity stands behind the world experienced by us and compels us in some way unknown to us to lead the manifoldness back to a unity. In that case we join thoughts without insight into the true basis of the connection that we bring about; then the truth is not known by us, but rather is forced upon us from outside. Let us call all science taking its start from this presupposition *dogmatic*. We will still have to come back to this.

Every scientific view of this kind will run into difficulty when it has to give reasons for why we make one or another connection between thoughts. It has to look around for a subjective basis for drawing objects together whose objective connection remains hidden to us. Why do I make a judgment, if the thing which demands that subject-concept and predicate-concept belong together has nothing to do with the making of this judgment?

Kant made this question the starting point of his critical work. At the beginning of his *Critique of Pure Reason* we find the question: How are synthetical judgments possible a priori?—this means, how is it possible for me to join two concepts (subject, predicate), if the content of the one is not already contained in the other, and if the judgment is not merely a perception-judgment, i.e., the establishing of an individual fact? Kant believes that such judgments are possible only if experience can exist only under the presumption of their validity. The possibility of experience is therefore the determining factor for us if we are to make a judgment of this kind. If I can say to myself that experience is possible only if one or another synthetical judgment is true a priori, only then is the judgment valid. But this does not apply to ideas themselves. For Kant these do not have even this degree of objectivity.

Kant finds that the principles of mathematics and of pure natural science are such *valid* synthetical principles a priori. He takes, for example, the principle that $7 + 5 = 12$. In 7 and 5 the sum 12 is in no way contained, concludes Kant. I must go beyond 7 and 5 and call upon my *intuition*; * then I find the concept 12. My intuition makes it necessary for me to picture that $7 + 5 = 12$. But the objects of my experience must approach me through the medium of my intuition, must submit to the laws of my intuition. If experience is to be possible, such principles must be correct.

This entire artificial thought-edifice of Kant does not stand up to objective examination. It is impossible that I have absolutely no point of reference in the subject-concept which leads me to the predicate-concept. For, both concepts were won by my intellect, and won from something that in itself is unified. Let us not deceive ourselves here. The mathematical unit that underlies the number is not primary. What is primary is the magnitude, which is so and so many repetitions of the unit. I must presuppose a magnitude when I speak of a unit. The unit is an entity of our intellect separated by the intellect out of a totality, in the same way that it distinguishes effect from cause, substance

* *Anschauung*— "Intuition" is the conventional translation of Kant's *Anschauung*.—Ed.

from its attributes, etc. Now, when I think 7 + 5, I am in fact grasping 12 mathematical units in thought, only not all at once, but rather in two parts. If I think the total of these mathematical units at one time, then that is exactly the same thing. And I express this identity in the judgment 7 + 5 = 12. It is exactly the same with the geometrical example Kant presents. A limited straight line with end points A and B is an indivisible unit. My intellect can form two concepts of it. On the one hand it can regard the straight line as *direction*, on the other as the *distance* between two points A and B. From this results the judgment that a straight line is the shortest distance between two points.

All judging, insofar as the parts entering into the judgment are concepts, is nothing more than a reuniting of what the intellect has separated. The connection reveals itself at once when one goes into the content of the concepts provided by the intellect.

13. The Activity of Knowing

Reality has separated itself for us into two realms: into experience and thinking. Experience comes into consideration in a twofold way. Firstly, insofar as all reality except thinking has a form of manifestation that must appear in the form of experience; and secondly, insofar as it lies in the nature of our spirit—whose being after all consists in *contemplation*, i.e., in an activity directed outward—that the objects to be observed must enter its field of vision, which is to say that they be given to it as experience. Now it could be the case that this form of the "given" does not contain the essential being *(Wesen)* of the thing, in which case the thing itself demands that it first manifest to perception (experience) in order later to reveal its essential being to an activity of our spirit that goes beyond perception. Another possibility is that the essential being is already present within the directly "given," and that it is only due to the second fact—that for our spirit everything must come before its gaze as experience—that we do not immediately become aware of this essential being. The latter is the case with thinking; the former is the case with the rest of reality. With thinking it is only necessary for us to overcome our own subjective limitations in order to grasp its core. What, with the rest of reality, is *factually* based in the objective perception—namely, that its immediate form of appearance must be overcome in order to explain it—this, with thinking, lies only in a peculiarity of our spirit. With the rest of reality, it is the thing itself that gives itself the form of experience; with thinking, it is the organization of our spirit. With the rest of reality, we do not have the whole thing when we grasp experience; with thinking we do.

Therein lies the basis of the dualism that science—the thinking activity of knowing—has to overcome. The human being finds himself confronted by two worlds whose connection he must establish. One of them is experience, about which he knows that it contains only half of reality; the other is thinking, which is complete in itself, and into which that outer perceptual reality must flow if a satisfying world view is to result. If the world were inhabited merely by sense beings, its essential being (its ideal content) would remain forever hidden; laws would indeed govern the processes of the world, but these laws would not come to manifestation. For these laws to come to manifestation, a being would have to insert itself between the phenomenal form and the law, a being to whom is given—in addition to the organs through which it perceives the sense-perceptible form of reality that is dependent upon the laws—also the ability to perceive the lawfulness itself. The sense world must approach such a being from one side, and the ideal essential being of the sense world from the other, and such a being must, in its own activity, unite these two factors of reality.

Here one sees perfectly well and clearly that our spirit is not to be regarded as a receptacle for the world of ideas, containing the thoughts within itself, but rather as an organ that perceives these thoughts.

It is an organ of apprehension in exactly the same way as eyes and ears are. A thought relates itself to our spirit in no other way than light does to the eye and sound to the ear. It certainly would not occur to anyone to regard color as something that imprints itself in a lasting way upon the eye, and, as it were, remains sticking to the eye. But with respect to the spirit this view is in fact the predominant one. A thought about each thing supposedly takes shape in consciousness, and this thought then remains in one's consciousness, in order to be taken out again when needed. One has based a whole theory on this, claiming that thoughts of which we are not for the moment conscious are in fact stored up within our spirit, but lying below the threshold of consciousness.

These fantastic views dissolve at once into nothing when one reflects that the world of ideas is after all determined out of itself. What does this self-determined content have to do with the multiplicity of consciousnesses? One will surely not assume that this content determines itself in indeterminate multiplicity in such a way that each partial content is always independent of the other! The matter is indeed utterly clear. The thought-content is such that absolutely all that is needed for it to manifest is a spiritual organ, but the number of beings endowed with this organ is of no significance. Any number of spirit-endowed individuals can therefore confront the *one* content of

67

thoughts. The human spirit, therefore, perceives the thought-content of the world as an organ of apprehension. There is only *one* thought-content of the world. Our consciousness is not the ability to produce and store up thoughts, as so many people believe, but rather the ability to perceive thoughts (ideas). Goethe expressed this aptly with the words: "The idea is eternal and single; that we also use the plural is not appropriate. All things of which we become aware and about which we are able to speak are only manifestations of the idea; concepts are what we express, and to this extent the idea itself is a concept."

As a citizen of two worlds—of the sense world and of the thought-world, the one pressing toward him from below, the other one shining from above—the human being takes possession of science, by which he joins the two into an undivided unity. From one side the outer form beckons to us, from the other side the inner essential being; we must unite the two. With this, our epistemology has lifted itself above the standpoint that similar investigations usually take and that does not get beyond formalism. One says that "the activity of knowing is to work upon experience," without specifying what it is that is worked into experience; the definition is set up that "in the activity of knowing, the perception flows into thinking, or that thinking, by virtue of an inner compulsion from experience, penetrates to the essential being behind experience." But this is mere formalism. A science of knowledge that wishes to grasp the activity of knowing in its universally significant role must first of all indicate its ideal purpose. This purpose consists of bringing incomplete experience to completion by revealing its core. Second, it must determine what this core is, with respect to content. This core is thought, idea. Third and last, it must show *how* this revealing takes place. Our chapter on

"Thinking and Perception" demonstrates this. Our epistemology leads to the positive conclusion that thinking is the essential being of the world and that individual (*individuelle*) human thinking is the individual (*einzelne*) form of manifestation of this essential being. A merely formalistic science of knowledge cannot do this; it remains forever unfruitful. It has no view about the nature of the relationship existing between what science gains and the essential being and processes of the world. And yet it is precisely within epistemology that this relationship must be found. This science must show us, after all, where we arrive through our knowing activity and where every other science leads us.

By no other path than epistemology does one come to the view that thinking is the core of the world. For, it shows us thinking's connection with the rest of reality. But out of what should we become aware of thinking's relationship to experience if not out of the science whose immediate aim is to investigate this relationship? And furthermore, how would we know that any spiritual or sense-perceptible being is the primal force of the world if we have not investigated its relationship to reality? If, therefore, we are ever concerned with discovering the essential being of something, this discovering always consists of going back to the ideal content of the world. One may not step outside the realm of this content if one wishes to remain within clear determinants and not grope about indeterminately. Thinking is a totality in itself, sufficient unto itself, that cannot overstep itself without entering a void. In other words, in order to explain something, thinking may not take refuge in things it does not find within itself. A thing not encompassed by thinking would be a non-thing. Everything ultimately merges with thinking; everything finds its place within thinking.

Expressed in terms of our individual consciousness, this means that, for the purpose of establishing anything scientifically, we must remain strictly within what is given us in consciousness; we cannot step outside of this. Now, if one recognizes fully that we cannot skip over our consciousness without landing in non-being, but does not recognize at the same time that the essential being of things is to be encountered in our consciousness in the perception of ideas, erroneous views then arise that speak of a limit to our knowledge. But if we cannot get outside our consciousness, and if the essential being of reality is not within it, then we cannot press forward to essential being at all.

Our thinking is bound to what is here and knows nothing of any beyond.

In our view, the opinion that there is a limit to knowledge is nothing but a thinking that misunderstands itself. A limit to knowledge would be possible only if outer experience in itself forced us to investigate its essential being, if *it* determined the questions that are to be raised in its presence. But this is not the case. For *thinking* the need arises to hold out, toward the experience of which it becomes aware, the essential being of this experience. After all, thinking can have only the quite definite tendency to see its own inherent lawfulness in the rest of the world, but not something or other about which it itself has not the least information.

Another error must still be rectified here. It is to the effect that thinking is not adequate to constitute the world, that some other factor (force, will, etc.) must still join with this thought-content in order to make the world possible.

Upon closer examination, however, one sees at once that all such factors turn out to be nothing more than abstractions from the perceptual world that are themselves awaiting explanation by thinking. Every other component

70

part of the being of the world except thinking would also require at once a kind of apprehension, a way of being known, different from that of thinking. We would have to reach that other component part in another way than through thinking. For, thinking yields only thoughts after all. But one is already contradicting oneself in wanting to explain the part played by that second component in world processes, and by making use of concepts in order to do so. Furthermore, however, there is no third element given us in addition to sense perception and thinking. And we cannot accept any part of sense perception as the core of the world, because, to closer scrutiny, all its components show that as such they do not contain their essential being. The essential being can therefore be sought simply and solely in thinking.

14. The Ground of Things and the Activity of Knowing

Kant, insofar as he directed the human being back upon himself, achieved a great step in philosophy. The human being should seek the grounds of certainty for his beliefs in what is given to him in his spiritual abilities and not in truths forced upon him from outside. Scientific conviction through oneself alone, that is the slogan of Kantian philosophy. He therefore called it above all a *critical* philosophy in contrast to a *dogmatic* one that receives fixed beliefs from tradition and afterward seeks proofs for them. With this, an antithesis of two scientific directions is given; but this antithesis was not thought through by Kant as keenly as it could have been.

Let us look more exactly at the way a scientific postulate can arise. A postulate joins two things: either a concept with a perception, or two concepts. A postulate of the latter kind is, for example: there is no effect without a cause. Now, the factual reasons for two concepts flowing together can lie beyond what they themselves contain and therefore beyond what alone is given me. I may then also have some formal reasons (logical consistency, particular axioms) for arriving at a particular combination of thoughts. But these have no influence upon the thing itself. The postulate rests upon something that I can never reach factually. A real insight into the thing is therefore not possible for me; I know about it only as an outsider. Here, what the postulate speaks of is in a world not known to me; the postulate alone is in my world. This is the nature of *dogma*. There are two kinds of dogma: the *dogma of revelation* and that of *experience*. The first kind passes down to man in one way or another truths about things that are withheld from his view. He has no insight into the world from which the postulates spring. He must *believe* in their truth; he has no access to their basis. The situation with the *dogma of experience* is quite similar. Someone who believes he should stick to bare, pure experience and can observe only its changes, without penetrating to its causal forces, is also setting up postulates about a world whose basis is inaccessible to him. Here too the truth is not attained through insight into the inner workings of the things, but rather is imposed by something external to the thing itself. Whereas the dogma of revelation ruled earlier science, present-day science suffers from the dogma of experience.

Our view has shown that any assumption about some ground of being that lies outside of the idea is nonsense. The entire ground of being has poured itself into the world and has merged with it. In thinking, the ground of being shows itself in its most perfect form, as it is in and for itself.

If thinking therefore makes a connection, forms a judgment, it is the very content of the ground of the world itself, having flowed into thinking, that is connected. In thinking, postulates are not given to us about some ground of the world in the beyond; rather the ground of the world, in its very substance, has flowed into thinking. We have direct insight into the factual grounds, not merely the formal grounds, for why a judgment takes place. The judgment does not determine anything about something foreign to it but only about its own content. Our view, therefore, establishes a true *knowing*. Our epistemology is really critical. According to our view, not only must nothing be allowed in, with respect to revelation, for which there are no factual grounds within thinking; but also experience must be recognized not only from the aspect of its manifestation, but also within thinking, as something causative. Through our thinking we lift ourselves from the view of reality as a *product* to a view of reality as something that *produces*.

Thus the essential being of a thing comes to light only when the thing is brought into relationship with the human being. For only within the human being does there manifest for each thing its essential being. This establishes relativism as a world view, that is, the direction in thought that assumes we see all things in the light bestowed upon them by human beings themselves. This view also bears the name anthropomorphism. It has many adherents. The majority of them, however, believe that this characteristic of our activity of knowing takes us away from objectivity as it is in and for itself. We perceive everything, so they believe, through the glasses of subjectivity. Our view shows us the exact opposite of this. We must look at things through these glasses if we want to come to their essential being. The world is not known to us only in the way it manifests to us, but rather it manifests as it is, although only to thinking contemplation. *The form of reality that the human being produces in science is the ultimate, true form of reality.*

Now it is still our task to extend into the individual realms of reality the way of knowing we have recognized as the correct one, i.e., the one that leads to the essential being of reality. We will now show *how*, in individual forms of experience, their essential being is to be sought.

E. THE ACTIVITY OF KNOWING NATURE

15. Inorganic Nature

Nature's simplest way of working seems to us to be that in which a process results entirely from factors that confront each other externally. Here, an event or relationship between two objects is not determined by an entity expressing itself in outer forms of manifestation, by an individuality that makes its inner abilities and character known by working outward. The event or relationship is called forth solely by the fact that one thing, in its workings, exercises a certain influence upon another, transferring its own conditions onto others. The conditions of the one thing then manifest as the consequence of those of the other. The system of processes occurring in this way—where one fact is always the result of other ones like it—is called inorganic nature.

Here, the course of a process, or that which is characteristic of a relationship, depends upon outer determinants; the facts bear attributes resulting from those determinants. If the way these outer factors interact changes, then of course the result of their interaction also changes; the phenomenon brought about in this way thus changes.

Now what is this interaction like in the case of inorganic nature as it directly enters our field of observation? It altogether bears the character we described above as that of *immediate experience*. Here we simply have to do with a particular case of that "experience in general." It is a matter here of connecting sense-perceptible facts. These connections, however, are precisely what manifest themselves to us so unclearly, so untransparently, in experience. One *fact* *a* confronts us, but at the same time numerous other ones do also. As we let our gaze sweep over the manifoldness presented here, we are totally in the dark as to which of the other facts have a closer relationship to this fact *a* and which have a more remote relationship. Some facts may be present without which the event cannot occur at all, and others are present that only modify it; without these the event could indeed occur, but would then, under different circumstances, assume a *different form*.

This also indicates the path that the activity of knowing has to take in this field. If the combination of facts in immediate experience does not suffice for us, then we must move on to a different combination that will satisfy our need for explanation. We have to create conditions such that a process will appear to us with transparent clarity as the necessary result of these conditions.

Let us recall why it is in fact that thinking, to direct experience, already contains its essential being. This is because we stand inside, not outside, the process that creates thought-connections between the individual thought-elements. Through this we are given not only the completed process, what has been effected, but also what is at work. And this is the point: in any occurrence of the outer world that confronts us, to see first of all the driving forces that bring this occurrence from the center of the world-all out into the periphery. The opaqueness and unclarity of a phenomenon or relationship in the sense world can be overcome only if we see, with total exactness, that it is the result of a *definite* constellation of facts. We must know that the process we see now arises through the working together of this and that element of the sense world. Then the way these elements interact must be completely penetrable by our intellect. The relationship into which the facts are brought must be an ideal one, one in accordance with our spirit. Naturally, within the relationships into which they are brought by the intellect, the things will behave in accordance with *their nature*.

We see at once what is gained by this. If I look at random into the sense world, I see processes brought about by the interaction of so many factors that it is impossible for me to see directly what actually stands as the effecting element behind these effects. I see a process and at the same time the facts $a, b, c,$ and d. How am I to know immediately which of these facts participate more in this process and which less? The matter becomes transparent if I first investigate which of the four facts are *absolutely* necessary for the process to occur at all. I find, for example that a and c

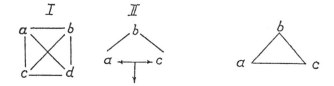

are absolutely necessary. I subsequently find that without d the process does indeed still occur, but significantly changed, whereas I see that b is of no essential significance and could be replaced by something else. In the above diagram, I is meant to represent symbolically the grouping of the elements for mere sense perception and II represents this grouping for the spirit. Our spirit, therefore, groups the facts of the inorganic world in such a way that it sees an event or a connection as the consequence of the facts' interrelationships. Thus our spirit brings necessity into what is of a chance nature. Let us make this clear through several examples. If I have a triangle $a \, b \, c$ before me, I definitely do not see at first glance that the sum of the three angles is always equal to a straight angle. This becomes clear immediately when I group the facts in the following way. From the two figures below it follows that angle *a'* equals angle *a*; angle *b'* equals angle *b*. (*AB* is parallel to *CD*; *A'B'* is parallel to *C'D'*). If I now have a triangle before me

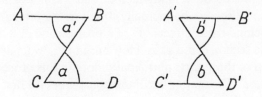

and draw a straight line parallel to *AB* through point *C*, I find, by using the above two figures, that angle *a'* equals angle *a*; angle *b'* equals angle *b*. Since *c* is equal to itself, the sum of the three angles of the triangle must equal a

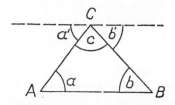

straight angle. Here I have explained a complicated combination of facts by leading it back to simple facts through which, from the relationship given to the human spirit, the corresponding connection follows necessarily from the nature of the given things.

Here is another example. I throw a stone in a horizontal direction. It follows a path we have represented by the line *l l'*. When I consider the driving forces that come into consideration here, I find: 1) the propelling force that I exert; 2) the force with which the earth draws the stone; 3) the force of air resistance.

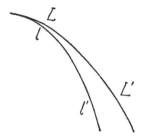

Upon further reflection I find that the first two forces are the *essential* ones, which determine the particular nature of the path, whereas the third force is secondary. If only the first two were at work, the stone would follow the path LL'. I find that path when I totally disregard the third force and bring only the first two into connection with each other. *Actually* performing this is neither possible nor necessary. I cannot eliminate all resistance. But I need only grasp in thought the nature of the first two forces, and then bring them into the necessary connection likewise only in thought, and the path L L' then results as the one that would necessarily have to result if only the two forces were working together.

In this way man's spirit reduces all the phenomena of inorganic nature into the kind of phenomena in which the effect appears to his spirit to emerge necessarily out of what is bringing about the effect.

If, after determining the stone's law of motion resulting from the first two forces one then brings in the third force also, the path l l' then results. Other determinants could complicate the matter still further. Every composite process of the sense world manifests as a web of such elementary facts interpenetrated by man's spirit and can be reduced to these.

Such a phenomenon, now, in which the character of the process follows directly and in a transparently clear way out of the nature of the pertinent factors, is called an *archetypal phenomenon (Urphänomen)* or a *basic fact (Grundtatsache)*.

This archetypal phenomenon is identical with objective natural law. For in it is expressed not only that a process has occurred under certain conditions but also that it had to occur. Given the nature of what was under consideration there, one *realizes* that the process had to occur. One demands outer empiricism so generally today because one believes that, with every assumption going beyond the empirically given, one is groping about in uncertainty. We see that we can remain completely *within* the phenomena and still arrive at what is necessary. The inductive method adhered to so much today can never do this. Basically, it proceeds in the following way. It sees a phenomenon that occurs in a particular way under the given conditions. A second time it sees the same phenomenon come about under similar conditions. From this it infers that a general law exists according to which this event must come about, and it expresses this law as such. Such a method remains totally outside the phenomena. It does not penetrate into the depths. Its laws are the generalizations of individual facts. It must always wait for confirmation of the rule by the individual facts. Our method knows that its laws are simply facts that have been wrested from the confusion of chance happening and made into necessary facts. We know that if the factors a and b are there, a particular effect must necessarily take place. We do not go outside the phenomenal world. The content of science, as we think of it, is nothing more than objective happening. Only the form according to which the facts are placed together is changed.

But through this one has actually penetrated a step deeper into objectivity than experience makes possible. We place facts together in such a way that they work in accordance with their own nature, and *only* in accordance with it, and this working is not modified by one circumstance or another.

We attach the greatest importance to the fact that these statements can be verified no matter where one looks in the real conduct of science. They are contradicted only by erroneous views held *about* the scope and nature of scientific principles. Whereas many of our contemporaries contradict *their own* theories when they enter the field of practical investigation, the harmony of all true investigation with our considerations could easily be shown in each individual case.

Our theory demands a definite form for every *law of nature*. It presupposes a complex of facts and determines that when this complex occurs anywhere in reality, a definite process must take place.

Every law of nature therefore has the form: When this fact interacts with that one, then this phenomenon arises. It would be easy to show that all laws of nature really have this form. When two bodies of differing temperature are touching each other, then warmth flows from the warmer one into the colder one until the temperature is the same in both. When there is a fluid in two containers connected to each other, the water level will be the same in both. When one object is standing between a source of light and another object, it will cast a shadow upon this other object. Whatever is not mere description in mathematics, physics, and mechanics must be *archetypal phenomenon*.

All progress in science depends upon becoming aware of archetypal phenomena. When one succeeds in lifting a process out of its connections with other ones and explaining it purely as the result of definite elements of experience, then one has penetrated a step deeper into the working of the world.

We have seen that the archetypal phenomenon presents itself purely in thoughts, when in thinking one relates the pertinent factors in accordance with their essential being. But one can also set up the necessary conditions artificially. This happens in scientific experiments. Here we have the occurrence of certain facts under our control. Of course we cannot disregard all circumstantial elements. But there is a means of getting around them. One produces a phenomenon with different modifications. One allows first these and then those circumstantial elements to work. A constant is then found to run through all these modifications. One must in fact retain what is essential in all the different combinations. One finds that in all these individual experiences one component part remains the same. This part is *higher experience* within experience. It is a *basic fact* or *archetypal phenomenon*.

Experimentation is meant to assure us that nothing influences a particular process except what we have taken into account. We bring together certain determining factors whose nature we know and wait to see what results. We have here an objective phenomenon on the basis of a subjective creation. We have something objective which at the same time is subjective through and through. *The experiment is therefore the true mediator between subject and object in inorganic science.*

The germ of the view we have developed here is to be found in Goethe's correspondence with Schiller. The letters between Goethe and Schiller from the beginning of 1798 concern themselves with this. They call this method *rational empiricism,* because it takes nothing other than objective processes as content for science; these objective processes, however, are held together by a web of concepts (laws) that our spirit discovers in them. Sense-perceptible processes in a connection with each other that can be grasped only by thinking—this is rational empiricism. If one compares those letters to Goethe's essay, "The Experiment as Mediator Between Subject and Object,"[7] one will see that the above theory follows consistently from them.

The general relationship we have established between experience and science therefore applies altogether to inorganic nature. Ordinary experience is only half of reality. For the senses, only this half is there. The other half is present only for our spiritual powers of apprehension. Our spirit lifts experience from being a *"manifestation for the senses"* to being a manifestation for the spirit itself. We have shown how it is possible in this field to lift oneself from what is caused to what is causing. Man's spirit finds the latter when his spirit approaches the former.

Scientific satisfaction from a view comes to us only when this view leads us into a totality complete in itself. Now the sense world in its inorganic aspect, however, does not show itself at any one point to be complete in itself; nowhere does there appear an individual wholeness. One process always directs us to another, upon which it depends; this one directs us to a third, and so on. Where is there any completion? In its inorganic aspect the sense world does not attain individuality. Only in its totality is it complete in itself. In order to have a wholeness, therefore, we must strive to grasp the entirety of the inorganic as *one* system. The cosmos is just such a system.

A penetrating understanding of the cosmos is the goal and ideal of inorganic science. Any scientific striving that does not push this far is mere preparation; it is a part of the whole, not the whole itself.

16. Organic Nature

For a long time science stopped short of entering the organic realm. It considered its methods to be insufficient for *understanding* life and its manifestations. It believed altogether, in fact, that all lawfulness such as that at work in inorganic nature ceased here. What was acknowledged to be the case in the inorganic world—that a phenomenon becomes comprehensible to us when we know its natural preconditions—was simply denied here. One thought of the organism as having been purposefully constructed according to a particular design of the creator. Every organ's use was supposedly predetermined; all questioning here could relate only to what the purpose of this or that organ might be, to why this or that is present. Whereas in the inorganic world one turned to the *pre*requisites of a thing, one considered these to be of no consequence at all for facts about life, and set the primary value on the *purpose* of a thing. With respect to the processes accompanying life one also did not ask, as in the case of physical phenomena, about the natural causes, but rather believed one had to ascribe these processes to a particular life force. One thought that what takes form there in the organism was the product of this force that simply disregards the other natural laws. Right up to the beginning of the nineteenth century science did not know how to deal with organisms. It was limited solely to the domain of the inorganic world.

Insofar as one sought the lawfulness of the organic, not in the nature of the objects but rather in the thought the creator follows in forming them, one also cut off any possibility of an explanation. How is that thought to become known to me? I am, after all, limited to what I have before me. If *this itself* does not reveal its laws to me within my thinking, then my scientific activity in fact comes to an end. There can be no question, in a *scientific sense*, of guessing the plans of a being standing outside. At the end of the eighteenth century the universally prevailing view was that there was no science to explain living phenomena in the sense in which physics, for example, is a science that explains things. Kant, in fact, tried to establish a philosophical basis for this view. He considered our intellect to be such that it could go only from the particular to the general. The particular, the individual, things are given to him, and from them he abstracts his general laws. Kant calls this kind of thinking "discursive," and considers it to be the only kind granted to the human being. Thus, in his view there is a science only for the kinds of things where the particular, taken in and for itself, is entirely without concept and is only summed up under an abstract concept. In the case of organisms Kant did not find this condition fulfilled. Here the single phenomenon betrays a *purposeful*, i.e., a *conceptual* arrangement. The particular bears traces of the concept. But, according to the Königsberg philosopher, we lack any ability to understand such beings. Understanding is possible for us only in the case where concept and individual thing are separated, where the concept represents something general, and the individual thing represents something particular. Thus there is nothing left us but to base our observations about organisms upon the *idea of purposefulness*: to treat living beings as though a system of intentions underlay their manifestation. Thus Kant has here established non-science scientifically, as it were.

Now Goethe protested vigorously against such unscientific conduct. He could never see why our thinking should not also be adequate to ask where an organ of a living being originates instead of what purpose it serves. Something in his nature always moved him to see every being in its inner completeness. It seemed to him an unscientific way of looking at things to bother only about the outer purposefulness of an organ, i.e., about its use for something other than itself. What should that have to do with the inner being of a thing? The point for him is never what purpose something serves but always *how* it *develops*. He does not want to consider an object as a thing complete in itself but rather in its becoming, so that he might know its origins. He was particularly drawn to Spinoza through the fact that Spinoza did not credit organs and organisms with outer *purposefulness*. For the activity of knowing the organic world, Goethe demanded a method that was scientific in exactly the same sense as the method we apply to the inorganic world.

Although not with as much genius as in Goethe, yet no less urgently, the need for such a method has arisen again and again in natural science. Today only a very small fraction of scientists doubt any longer the possibility of this method. Whether the attempts made here and there to introduce such a method have succeeded is, to be sure, another question.

Above all, one has committed a serious error in this. One believed that the method of inorganic science should simply be taken over into the realm of organisms. One considered the method employed here to be altogether the only scientific one, and thought that for "*organics*" to be scientifically possible, it would have to be so in exactly the same sense in which *physics* is, for example. The possibility was forgotten, however, that perhaps the concept of what is

86

scientific is much broader than "the explanation of the world according to the laws of the physical world." Even today one has not yet penetrated through to this knowledge. Instead of investigating what it is that makes the approach of the inorganic sciences scientific, and of then seeking a method that can be applied to the world of living things while adhering to the requirements that result from this investigation, one simply declared that the laws gained upon this lower stage of existence are universal.

Above all, however, one should investigate what the basis is for any scientific thinking. We have done this in our study. In the preceding chapter we have also recognized that inorganic lawfulness is not the only one in existence but is only a special case of all possible lawfulness in general. The method of physics is simply one *particular* case of a general scientific way of investigation in which the nature of the pertinent objects and the region this science serves are taken into consideration. If this method is extended into the organic, one obliterates the specific nature of the organic. Instead of investigating the organic in accordance with its nature, one forces upon it a lawfulness alien to it. In this way, however, by denying the organic, one will never come to know it. Such scientific conduct simply repeats, upon a higher level, what it has gained upon a lower one; and although it believes that it is bringing the higher form of existence under laws established elsewhere, this form slips away from it in its efforts, because such scientific conduct does not know how to grasp and deal with this form in its particular nature.

All this comes from the erroneous view that the method of a science is extraneous to its objects of study, that it is not determined by these objects but rather by *our* own nature. It is believed that one must think in a particular way about objects, that one must indeed think about *all* objects—throughout the entire universe—in the same way. Investigations are undertaken that are supposed to show that, due to the nature of our spirit, we can think only inductively or deductively, etc.

In doing so, however, one overlooks the fact that the objects perhaps will not tolerate the way of looking at them that we want to apply to them.

A look at the views of Haeckel, who is certainly the most significant of the natural-scientific theoreticians of the present day, shows us that the objection we are making to the organic natural science of our day is entirely justified: namely, that it does not carry over into organic nature the principle of scientific contemplation in the absolute sense, but only the principle of inorganic nature.

When he demands of all scientific striving that "the *causal* interconnections of phenomena become recognized everywhere," when he says that "if *psychic mechanics* were not so infinitely complex, if we were also able to have a complete overview of the historical development of psychic functions, we would then be able to bring them all into a mathematical soul formula," then one can see clearly from this what he wants: *to treat the whole world according to the stereotype of the method of the physical sciences.*

This demand, however, does not underlie Darwinism in its original form but only in its present-day interpretation. We have seen that to explain a process in inorganic nature means to show its *lawful emergence* out of other sense-perceptible realities, to trace it back to objects that, like *itself,* belong to the sense world. But how does modern organic science employ the principles of *adaptation* and the *struggle for existence* (both of which we certainly do not doubt are the expression of facts)? It is believed that one can trace

88

the character of a particular species directly back to the outer conditions in which it lived, in somewhat the same way as the heating of an object is traced back to the rays of the sun falling upon it. One forgets completely that one can never show a species' character, with all its qualities that are full of content, to be the result of these conditions. The conditions may have a determining influence, but they are not a *creating* cause. We can definitely say that under the influence of certain circumstances a species had to evolve in such a way that one or another organ became particularly developed; what is there as content, however, the specifically organic, cannot be derived from outer conditions. Let us say that an organic entity has the essential characteristics *a b c*; then, under the influence of certain outer conditions, it has evolved. Through this, its characteristics have taken on the particular form *a' b' c'*. When we take these influences into account we will then understand that *a* has evolved into the form of *a'*, *b* into *b'*, *c* into *c'*. But the specific nature of *a, b,* and *c* can never arise as the outcome of external conditions.

One must, above all, focus one's thinking on the question: From what do we then derive the content of that general "something" of which we consider the individual organic entity to be a specialized case? We know very well that the specialization comes from external influences. But we must trace the specialized shape itself back to an inner principle. We gain enlightenment as to why just this particular form has evolved when we study a being's environment. But this particular form is, after all, something in and of itself; we see that it possesses certain characteristics. We see what is essential. A content, configured in itself, confronts the outer phenomenal world, and this content provides us with what we need in tracing those characteris-

89

tics back to their source. In inorganic nature we perceive a fact and see, in order to explain it, a second, a third fact and so on; and the result is that the first fact appears to us to be the necessary consequence of the other ones. In the organic world this is not so. There, in addition to the facts, we need yet another factor. We must see what works in from outer circumstances as confronted by something that does not passively allow itself to be determined by them but rather determines itself, actively, out of itself, under the influence of the outer circumstances.

But what is that basic factor? It can, after all, be nothing other than what manifests in the particular in the *form of the general*. In the particular, however, a definite organism always manifests. That basic factor is therefore an organism in the form of the general: a *general image of the organism*, which comprises within itself all the particular forms of organisms.

Following Goethe's example, let us call this general organism *typus*. Whatever the word *typus* might mean etymologically, we are using it in this Goethean sense and never mean anything else by it than what we have indicated. This *typus* is not developed in all its completeness in any single organism. Only our thinking, in accordance with reason, is able to take possession of it, by drawing it forth, as a general image, from phenomena. The *typus* is therewith the idea of the organism: the animalness in the animal, the general plant in the specific one.

One should not picture this *typus* as anything rigid. It has nothing at all to do with what Agassiz, Darwin's most significant opponent, called "an incarnate creative thought of God's." The *typus* is something altogether fluid, from which all the particular species and genera, which one can regard as subtypes or specialized types, can be derived. The *typus* does not preclude the theory of evolution. It does not contradict the *fact* that organic forms evolve out of one another. It is only reason's protest against the view that organic development consists purely in sequential, factual (sense-perceptible) forms. It is what underlies this whole development. It is what establishes the interconnection in all this endless manifoldness. It is the inner aspect of what we experience as the outer forms of living things. *The Darwinian theory presupposes the typus.*

The *typus* is the true archetypal organism; according to how it specializes ideally, it is either archetypal plant or archetypal animal. It cannot be any one, sense-perceptibly real living being. What Haeckel or other naturalists regard as the archetypal form is already a particular shape; it is, in fact, the simplest shape of the *typus*. The fact that in time the *typus* arises in its simplest form first does not require the forms arising later to be the result of those preceding them in time. *All* forms result as a *consequence of the typus*; the first as well as the last are manifestations of it. We must take it as the basis of a true organic science and not simply undertake to derive the individual animal and plant species *out* of one another. The *typus* runs like a red thread through all the developmental stages of the organic world. We must hold onto it and then *with it* travel through this great realm of many forms. Then this realm will become understandable to us. Otherwise it falls apart for us, just as the rest of the world of experience does, into an unconnected mass of particulars. In fact, even when we believe that we are leading what is later, more complicated, more compound, back to a *previous* simpler form and that in the latter we have something original, even then we are deceiving ourselves, for we have only derived a specific form from a specific form.

Friedrich Theodor Vischer once said of the Darwinian theory that it necessitates a revision of our concept of time. We have now arrived at a point that makes evident to us in what sense such a revision would have to occur. It would have to show that deriving something later out of something earlier is no explanation, that what is first in time is not first in principle. All deriving has to do with principles, and at best it could be shown which factors were at work such that one species of beings evolved *before* another one *in time*.

The *typus* plays the same role in the organic world as natural law does in the inorganic. Just as natural law provides us with the possibility of recognizing each individual occurrence as a part of one great whole, so the *typus* puts us in a position to regard the individual organism as a particular form of the archetypal form.

We have already indicated that the *typus* is not a completed frozen conceptual form, but that it is fluid, that it can assume the most manifold configurations. The number of these configurations is infinite, because that through which the archetypal form is a single particular form has no significance for the archetypal form itself. It is exactly the same as the way one law of nature governs infinitely many individual phenomena, because the specific conditions that arise in an individual case have nothing to do with the law.

Nevertheless, we have to do here with something essentially different than in inorganic nature. There it was a matter of showing that a particular sense-perceptible fact can occur in this and in no other way, because this or that *natural law* exists. The fact and the law confront each other as two separate factors, and absolutely no further spiritual work is necessary except, when we become aware of a fact, to remember the law that applies. This is different in the case of a living being and its manifestations. Here it is a matter of developing, out of the *typus* that we must have grasped, the individual form arising in our experience. We must carry out a spiritual process of an essentially different kind. We may not simply set the *typus*, as something finished in the way the natural law is, over against the individual phenomenon.

The fact that every object, if it is not prevented by incidental circumstances, falls to the earth in such a way that the distances covered in successive intervals of time are in the ratio 1:3:5:7, etc., is a definite *law* that is fixed once and for all. It is an *archetypal phenomenon* that occurs when two masses (the earth and an object upon it) enter into interrelationship. If now a specific case enters the field of our observation to which this law is applicable, we then need only look at the facts observable to our senses in the connection with which the law provides us, and we will find this law to be confirmed. We lead the individual case back to the law. The natural law expresses the connection of the facts that are separated in the sense world; but it continues to exist as such over against the individual phenomenon. With the *typus* we must *develop* the particular case confronting us *out of* the archetypal form. We may not place the *typus* over against the individual form in order to see how it governs the latter; we must allow the individual form to *go forth* out of the *typus*. A law governs the phenomenon as something standing over it; the *typus* flows into the individual living being; it identifies itself with it.

If an organic science wants to be a science in the sense that mechanics or physics is, it must therefore know the *typus* to be the most general form and must then show it also in diverse, ideal, separate shapes. Mechanics is indeed also a compilation of diverse natural laws where the real determinants are altogether hypothetically assumed. It must be no different in organic science. Here also one would have to assume hypothetically determined forms in which the *typus* develops itself if one wanted to have a rational science. One would then have to show how these hypothetical configurations can always be brought to a definite form *that exists* for our observation.

Just as in the inorganic we lead a phenomenon back to a law, so here we *develop* a specific form out of the archetypal form. Organic science does not come about by outwardly juxtaposing the general and the particular, but rather by developing the one form out of the other.

Just as mechanics is a system of natural laws, so organic science is meant to be a series of developmental forms of the *typus*. It is just that in mechanics we must bring the individual laws together and *order* them into a *whole*, whereas here we must allow the individual forms to go forth from one another in a living way.

It is possible to make an objection here. If the *typical* form is something altogether fluid, how is it at all possible to set up a chain of sequential, particular types as the content of an organic science? One can very well picture to oneself that, in every particular case one observes, one recognizes a specific form of the *typus*, but one cannot, after all, for the purposes of science merely collect such real observed cases.

One can do something else, however. One can let the *typus* run through its series of possibilities and then always (hypothetically) hold fast to this or that form. In this way one gains a series of forms, derived in thought from the *typus*, as the content of a *rational organic science*.

An organic science is possible which, like mechanics, is science in altogether the strictest sense. It is just that the method is a different one. The method of mechanics is to prove things. Every proof is based upon a certain principle. There always exists a particular presupposition (i.e., potentially experienceable conditions are indicated), and it is then determined what happens when these presuppositions occur. We then understand the individual phenomenon by applying the underlying law. We think about it like this: Under these conditions, a phenomenon occurs; the conditions are there, so the phenomenon *must* occur. This is our thought process when we approach an event in the inorganic world in order to explain it. This is the method that proves things. It is scientific because it completely permeates a phenomenon with a concept, because, through it, perception and thinking coincide.

But we can do nothing with this proving method in organic science. The *typus*, in fact, does not bring it about that under certain conditions a particular phenomenon will occur; it determines nothing about a relationship of parts that are alien to each other, that confront each other externally. It determines only the lawfulness of *its* own parts. It does not point, like a natural law, beyond itself. The particular organic forms can therefore be *developed* only out of the *general typus form*, and the organic beings that arise in experience must coincide with one such derivative form of the *typus*. The developmental method must here take the place of the proving one. One establishes here not that outer conditions affect each other in a certain way and thereby have a definite result, but rather that under definite outer circumstances a particular form has developed out of the *typus*. This is the far-reaching difference between inorganic and organic science. This difference underlies no investigative approach as consistently as the Goethean one. No one has recognized better than Goethe that an organic science, without any dark mysticism, without teleology, without assuming special creative thoughts, must be possible. But also, no one has more vigorously rejected the unwarranted expectation of being able to accomplish anything here with the methods of inorganic science.[8]

The *typus*, as we have seen, is a fuller scientific form than the archetypal phenomenon. It also presupposes a more intensive activity of our spirit than the archetypal phenomenon does. As we reflect upon the things of inorganic nature, sense perception supplies us with the content. Our sense organization already supplies us here with that which in the organic realm we receive only through our spirit. In order to perceive sweet, sour, warmth, cold, light, color, etc., one need only have healthy senses. We have only to find, *in thinking*, the form for the matter. In the *typus*, however, content and form are closely bound to each other. Therefore the *typus* does not in fact determine the content purely formally the way a law does but rather permeates the content livingly, from within outward, as its own. Our spirit is confronted with the task of participating productively in the creation of the content along with the formal element.

The kind of thinking in which the content appears in direct connection with the formal element has always been called *"intuitive."*

Intuition appears repeatedly as a scientific principle. The English philosopher Reid calls it an intuition if, out of our perception of outer phenomena (sense impressions), we were to acquire at the same time a conviction that they really *exist*. Jacobi thought that in our feeling of God we are given not only this feeling itself but at the same time the proof that God *is*. This judgment is also called intuitive. What is characteristic of intuition, as one can see, is always that more is given in the content than this content itself; one knows about a thought-characterization, *without proof*, merely through direct conviction. One believes it to be unnecessary to prove one's thought-characterizations ("real existence," etc.) about the material of perception; in fact, one possesses them in unseparated unity with the content. With the *typus* this is really the case. Therefore it can offer no means of proof but can merely provide the possibility of developing every particular form out of itself. Our spirit, consequently, must work much more intensively in grasping the *typus* than in grasping a natural law. It must produce the content along with the form. It must take upon itself an activity that the senses carry out in inorganic science and that we call beholding *(Anschauung)*. At this higher level, the spirit itself must therefore be able to behold. Our power of judgment must be a *thinking beholding*, and a *beholding thinking*. We have to do here, as was expounded for the first time by Goethe, with a power to judge in beholding *(anschauende Urteilskraft)*. Goethe thereby revealed as a necessary form of apprehension in the human spirit that which Kant wanted to prove was something the human being, by his whole make-up, is not granted.

Just as in organic nature the *typus* takes the place of the natural law (archetypal phenomenon) of inorganic nature, so intuition (the power to judge in beholding) takes the place of the proving (reflecting) power of judgment. Just as one believed that one could apply to organic nature the same laws that pertain to a lower stage of knowledge, so also one supposed that the same methods are valid here as there. Both are errors.

One has often treated intuition in a very belittling way in science. One regarded it as a defect in Goethe's spirit that he wanted to attain scientific truths by intuition. What is attained in an intuitive way is, in fact, considered by many to be quite important when it is a matter of a scientific *discovery*. There, one says, an *inspiration* often leads further than a methodically trained thinking. One frequently calls it intuition, in fact, when someone by chance has hit upon something right, whose truth the researcher must first convince himself of by roundabout means. But it is always denied that intuition itself could be a principle of science. What occurs to intuition must afterward first be proved— so it is thought—if it is to have any scientific value.

Thus one also considered Goethe's scientific achievements to be brilliant inspirations that only afterward received credibility through strict science.

But for organic science, intuition is the right method. It follows quite clearly from our considerations, we think, that Goethe's spirit found the right path in the organic realm precisely because it was intuitively predisposed. The method appropriate to the organic realm coincided with the constitution of his spirit. Because of this it only became all the more clear to him the extent to which this method differs from that of inorganic science. The one became clear to him through the other. He therefore could also sketch the nature of the inorganic in clear strokes.

The belittling way in which intuition is treated is due in no small measure to the fact that one believes the same degree of credibility cannot be attributed to its achievements as to those of the proving sciences. One often calls *"knowing"* only that which has been proved, and everything else *"faith."*

One must bear in mind that intuition means something completely different within *our* scientific direction—which is convinced that in thinking we grasp the core of the world in its essential being—than in that direction which shifts this core into a beyond we cannot investigate. A person who sees in the world lying before us—insofar as we either experience it or penetrate it with our thinking—nothing more than a reflection (an image of some other-worldly, unknown, active principle that remains hidden behind this shell not only to one's *first glance* but also to all scientific investigation) such a person can certainly regard the proving method as nothing but a substitute for the insight we lack into the *essential being* of things. Since he does not press through to the view that a thought-connection comes about directly through the *essential* content given in thought, i.e., through the thing itself, he believes himself able to support this thought-connection only through the fact that it is in harmony with several basic convictions (axioms) so simple that they are neither susceptible to proof nor in need thereof. If such a person is then presented with a scientific statement without proof, a statement, indeed, that by its very nature excludes the proving method, then it seems to him to be imposed from outside. A truth approaches him without his knowing what the basis of its validity is. He believes he has no knowledge, no *insight* into the matter; he believes he can only give himself over to the *faith* that, *outside his powers of thought*, some basis or other for its validity exists.

Our world view is in no danger of having to regard the limits of the proving method as at the same time the limits of scientific conviction. It has led us to the view that the core of the world flows into our thinking, that we do not think *about* the essential being of the world, but rather that thinking is a merging with the essential being of reality. With intuition a truth is not imposed upon us from outside, because, from our standpoint, there *is* no inner and outer in the sense assumed by the scientific direction just characterized and that is in opposition to our own. For us, intui-

99

tion is a direct being-within, a penetrating into the truth that gives us everything that pertains to it at all. It merges completely with what is given to us in our intuitive judgment. The essential characteristic of *faith* is totally absent here, which is that only the finished truth is given us and not its basis and that penetrating insight into the matter under consideration is denied us. The insight gained on the path of intuition is just as scientific as the proven insight.

Every single organism is the development of the *typus* into a particular form. Every organism is an individuality that governs and determines itself from a center. It is a self-enclosed whole, which in inorganic nature is only the case with the *cosmos*.

The ideal of inorganic science is to grasp the totality of all phenomena as a unified system, so that we approach every phenomenon with the consciousness of recognizing it as a part of the cosmos. In organic science, on the other hand, the ideal must be, in the *typus* and in its forms of manifestation, to have with the greatest possible perfection what we see *develop* in the sequence of single beings. Leading the *typus* through all the phenomena is what matters here. In inorganic science it is the *system*; in organic science it is *comparison* (of each individual form with the *typus*).

Spectral analysis and the perfecting of astronomy are extending out to the universe the truths gained in the limited region of the earth. They are thereby approaching the first ideal. The second ideal will be fulfilled when *the comparing method employed by Goethe* is recognized in all its implications.

F. THE HUMANITIES*

17. Introduction: Spirit and Nature

We have now dealt fully with the realm of knowledge of nature. Organic science is the highest form of natural science. It is the humanities that go beyond it. These demand an essentially different approach of the human spirit to its object of study than the natural sciences. In the latter the human spirit had to play a universal role. The task fell to the human spirit to bring the world process itself to a conclusion, so to speak. What existed there without the human spirit was only half of reality, was unfinished, was everywhere patchwork. The task of the human spirit there is to call into manifest existence the innermost mainsprings of reality, which, to be sure, would be operative even without its subjective intervention. If man were a mere sense being, without spiritual comprehension, inorganic nature would certainly be no less dependent upon natural laws, but these, as such, would never come into existence. Beings would indeed then exist that perceived what is brought about (the sense world) but not what is bringing about (the inner lawfulness). It is really the genuine and indeed the truest form of nature that comes to manifestation within the human spirit, whereas for a mere sense being only nature's outer side is present. Science has a role of universal significance here. It is the conclusion of the work of creation. It is nature's coming to terms with itself that plays itself out in man's consciousness. Thinking is the final part in the sequence of processes that compose nature.

It is not like this with the humanities. Here our consciousness has to do with spiritual content itself: with the

---

* *Geisteswissenschaften,* "spiritual sciences," i.e., sciences dealing with the human spirit.—Ed.

individual human spirit, with creations of culture, of literature, with successive scientific convictions, with creations of
art. The spiritual is grasped by the spirit. Here, reality already has within itself the ideal element, the lawfulness, that
otherwise emerges only in spiritual apprehension. That
which in the natural sciences is only the product of reflection about the objects is here innate in them. Science plays
a different role here. The *essential being* would already be
in the object even without the work of science. It is human
deeds, creations, ideas with which we have to do here. It is
man's coming to terms with himself and with his race.
Science has a different mission to fulfill here than it does
with respect to nature.

Again this mission arises first of all as a human need.
Just as the necessity of finding the idea of nature corresponding to the reality of nature arises first of all as a need
of our spirit, so the task of the humanities is there first of
all as a human impulse. Again it is only an objective fact
manifesting as a subjective need.

Man should not, like a being of inorganic nature, work
upon another being in accordance with outer norms, in accordance with a lawfulness *governing* him; he should also
not be merely the individual form of a general *typus*; rather
he himself should set himself the purpose, the goal of his
existence, of his activity. If his actions are the results of
laws, then these laws must be such that he gives them to
himself. What he is in himself, what he is among his own
kind, within the state and in history, this he should not be
through external determining factors. *He must be this*
through himself. How he fits himself into the structure of
the world depends upon him. He must find the point where
he can participate in the workings of the world. Here the
humanities receive their task. The human being must know

the spiritual world in order to determine his part in it according to this knowledge. The mission that psychology, ethnology, and history have to fulfill springs from this.

It is in inherent in the being of *nature* for law and activity to separate from each other, for the latter to manifest as governed by the former; on the other hand, it is inherent in the being of our *spiritual activity (Freiheit)** for law and activity to coincide, for what is acting to present itself directly in what is enacted, and for what is enacted to govern itself.

The humanities are therefore pre-eminently sciences of our spiritual activity (Freiheitswissenschaften). The idea of spiritual activity must be their centerpoint, the idea that governs them. This is why Schiller's *Aesthetic Letters* have such stature, because they want to find the essential being of beauty in the idea of spiritual activity, because spiritual activity is the principle that imbues them.

The human spirit is able to assume only that place in the generality of the world, in the cosmic whole, that it gives itself as an individual spirit. Whereas in organic science the general, the idea of the *typus*, must always be kept in view, in the humanities the idea of the personality must be maintained. What matters here is not the idea as it presents itself in a general form *(typus)* but rather the idea as it arises in the single being (individual). Of course the important thing is not the chance, single personality, not this or that personality, but rather *personality as such*; not personality as it develops out of itself into particular forms and then first comes in this way into sense-perceptible existence, but rather personality sufficient within itself, complete in itself, finding within itself its own determinative elements.

* Rudolf Steiner suggested "spiritual activity" as a translation of the German word *Freiheit* (literally, "freehood"). For him, *Freiheit* meant "action, thinking, and feeling from out of the spiritual individuality of man."—Ed.

It is determinative for the *typus* that it can only first realize itself in the individual being. It is determinative for a person that he attain an existence which, already ideal, is really self-sustaining. It is completely different to speak of a general humanity than of a general lawfulness of nature. With the latter the particular is determined by the general; with the idea of humanity the generality is determined by the particular. If we succeed in discerning general laws in history, these are laws only insofar as historic personalities placed them before themselves as goals, as ideals. This is the inner antithesis of nature and the human spirit. Nature demands a science that ascends from the directly given, as the *caused*, to what the human spirit can grasp, as *that which causes*; the human spirit demands a science that progresses from the given, as *that which causes*, to the *caused*. What characterizes the humanities is that the *particular* is what gives the laws; what characterizes the natural sciences is that this role falls to the general.

What is of value to us in natural science only as a transitional point—the particular—is alone of interest to us in the humanities. What we seek in natural science—the *general*—comes into consideration here only insofar as it elucidates the *particular* for us.

It would be contrary to the spirit of science if, with respect to nature, one stopped short at the direct experience of the particular. But it would also mean positive death to the spirit if one wanted to encompass Greek history, for example, in a general conceptual schema. In the first case our attention, clinging to the phenomena, would not achieve science; in the second case our spirit, proceeding in accordance with a general stereotype, would lose all sense of what is individual.

104

18. Psychological Knowing Activity

The first science in which the human spirit has to do with itself is psychology. The human spirit confronts itself, contemplating.

Fichte allowed existence to the human being only insofar as he himself posits this existence within himself. In other words, the human personality has only those traits, characteristics, capacities, etc., that, by virtue of insight into its essential being, it ascribes to itself. A person would not recognize as his own a human capacity about which he knew nothing; he would attribute it to something foreign to him. When Fichte supposed that he could found all the science of the universe upon this truth, he was in error. But it is suited to become the highest principle of psychology. It determines the method of psychology. If the human spirit possesses a quality only insofar as this spirit attributes it to itself, then the psychological method is the penetration of the human spirit into its own activity. Self-apprehension is therefore the method here.

We are, of course, not limiting psychology to being a science of the chance characteristics of any one human individual. We are disengaging the individual spirit from its chance limitations, from its secondary features, and are seeking to raise ourselves to the contemplation of the human individual as such.

To contemplate the entirely chance single individual is not, in fact, the important thing, but rather to become clear about the individual as such, which determines itself out of itself. If someone were to say in response to this that here too we are dealing with nothing more than the *typus* of mankind, he would be confusing the *typus* with a generalized concept. It is essential to the *typus* that it stand as something general over against its individual forms. This is not essential to the concept of the human individual. Here the general is directly active in the individual being, but this activity expresses itself in different ways according to the objects upon which it focuses. The *typus* presents itself in individual forms and in *these* enters into interaction with the outer world. The human spirit has only one form. But in one situation certain objects stir his feelings, in another an ideal inspires him to act, etc. We are not dealing with a particular form of the human spirit; but always with the whole and complete human being. We must separate him from his surroundings if we wish to understand him. If one wishes to attain the *typus*, then one must ascend from the single form to the archetypal form; if one wishes to attain the human spirit one must disregard the outer manifestations through which it expresses itself, disregard the specific actions it performs, and look at it in and for itself. We must observe it to see how it acts in general, not how it has acted in this or that situation. In the *typus* one must separate the general form by comparison out of the individual forms; in psychology one must merely separate the individual form from its surroundings.

In psychology it is no longer the case, as in organic science, that we recognize in the particular being a configuration of the general, of the archetypal form; rather we recognize the perception of the particular as this archetypal form itself. The human spirit being is not *one* configuration of its idea but rather *the* configuration of its idea. When Jacobi believes that at the same time as we gain perception of our inner life we attain the conviction that a unified being underlies it (intuitive self-apprehension), he is in error, because in fact we perceive this unified being itself. What otherwise is intuition in fact becomes self-observation here. With regard to the highest form of existence this is also an

106

objective necessity. What the human spirit can garner from the phenomena is the highest form of content that it can attain at all. If the human spirit then reflects upon itself, it must recognize itself as the direct manifestation of this highest form, as the bearer of this highest form. What the human spirit finds as unity in manifold reality it must find in the human spirit's singleness as direct existence. What it places, as something general, over against the particular it must ascribe to its own individuality as the essential being of this individuality itself.

One can see from all this that a true psychology can be achieved only if one studies the nature of the human spirit as an active entity. In our time one has wanted to replace this method by another which considers psychology's object of study to be the phenomena in which the human spirit presents itself rather than *this spirit itself.* One believes that the individual expressions of the human spirit can be brought into external relationships just as much as the facts of inorganic nature can. In this way one wants to found a "theory of the soul without any soul." Our study shows, however, that with this method one loses sight of the very thing that matters. One should separate the human spirit from its various expressions and return to this spirit itself as the producer of them. One usually limits oneself to the expressions and forgets the spirit. Here also one has allowed oneself to be led astray to succumb to that incorrect standpoint that wants to apply the methods of mechanics, physics, etc., to all sciences.

The unified soul is given to us in experience just as much as its individual actions are. Everyone is aware of the fact that his thinking, feeling, and willing proceed from his "I." Every activity of our personality is connected with this center of our being. If one disregards this connection with the personality in an action, then the action ceases to be an expression of the soul at all. It falls either under the concept of inorganic or of organic nature. If two balls are lying on the table and I propel one against the other, then, if one disregards my intention and my will, everything is reduced to physical or physiological processes. The main thing with all manifestations of the human spirit—thinking, feeling, and willing—is to recognize them in their essential being as expressions of the personality. Psychology is based on this.

But the human being does not belong only to himself; he also belongs to society. What lives and manifests in him is not merely his individuality but also that of the nation to which he belongs. What he accomplishes emerges just as much out of the full strength of his people as out of his own. With his mission he also fulfills a part of the mission of the larger community of his people. The point is for his place within his people to be such that he can bring to full expression the strength of his individuality. This is possible only if the social organism is such that the individual is able to find the place where he can set to work. It must not be left to chance whether he finds this place or not.

It is the task of ethnology and political science to investigate how the individual lives and acts within the social community. The individuality of peoples is the subject of this science. It has to show what form the organism of the state has to assume if the individuality of a people is to come to expression in it. The constitution a people gives itself must be developed out of its innermost being. In this domain also, errors of no small scope are in circulation. One does not regard political science as an experiential science. It is believed that all peoples can set up a constitution according to a certain model.

108

The constitution of a people, however, is nothing other than its individual character brought into a definite form of laws. A person who wants to predetermine the direction a particular activity of a people has to take must not impose anything upon it from outside; he must simply express what lies unconsciously within the character of his people. "It is not the intelligent person that rules, but rather intelligence; not the reasonable person, but rather reason," says Goethe.

To grasp the individuality of a people as a reasonable one is the method of ethnology. The human being belongs to a whole, whose nature is an organization of reason. Here again we can quote a statement of Goethe's: "The rational world is to be regarded as a great immortal individual that unceasingly brings about the necessary, and through doing so in fact makes itself master over chance." Just as psychology has to investigate the nature of the single individual, so ethnology (the psychology of peoples) has to investigate that "immortal individual."

19. Human Spiritual Activity *(Freiheit)*

Our view about the sources of our knowing activity cannot help but affect the way we view our practical conduct. The human being does indeed act in accordance with thought-determinants that lie within him. What he does is guided by the intentions and goals he sets himself. But it is entirely obvious that these goals, intentions, ideals, etc., will bear the same character as the rest of man's thought-world. Dogmatic science will therefore offer a truth for human conduct of an essentially different character than that resulting from our epistemology. If the truths the human being attains in science are determined by a factual necessity having its seat outside thinking, then the ideals upon which he bases his actions will also be determined in the same way. The human being then acts in accordance with laws he cannot verify objectively: he imagines some norm that is prescribed for his actions from outside. But this is the nature of any *commandment* that the human being has to observe. Dogma, as principle of conduct, is moral commandment.

With our epistemology as a foundation, the matter is quite different. Our epistemology recognizes no other foundation for truths than the thought content lying within them. When a moral ideal comes about, therefore, it is the inner power lying within the content of this ideal that guides our actions. It is not because an ideal is given us as law that we act in accordance with it, but rather because the ideal, by virtue of its content, is active in us, leads us. The stimulus to action does not lie outside of us; it lies *within* us. In the case of a commandment of duty we would feel ourselves subject to it; we would have to act in a particular way because it ordered us to do so. There, "should" comes first and then "want to," which must submit itself to the "should." According to our view, this is not the case. Man's willing is sovereign. It carries out only what lies as thought-content within the human personality. The human being does not let himself be given laws by any outer power; he is his own lawgiver.

And, according to our world view, who, in fact, should give them to him? The ground of the world has poured itself completely out into the world; it has not withdrawn from the world in order to guide it from outside; it drives the world from inside; it has not withheld itself from the world. The highest form in which it arises within the reality of ordinary life is thinking and, along with thinking, the human personality. If, therefore, the world ground has goals, they are identical with the goals that the human being

110

sets himself in living and in what he does. It is not by searching out this or that commandment of the guiding power of the world that he acts in accordance with its intentions but rather through acting in accordance with his own insights. For within these insights there lives that guiding power of the world. It does not live as will somewhere outside the human being; it has given up all will of its own in order to make everything dependent upon man's will. In order for the human being to be able to be his own lawgiver, he must give up all thoughts of such things as extra-human determining powers of the world, etc.

Let us take this opportunity to call attention to the excellent article by Kreyenbühl in *Philosophische Monatshefte*, vol.18, no.3, 1882.* This explains correctly how the maxims for our actions result altogether from the direct determinations of our individuality; how everything that is ethically great is not imposed by the power of moral law but rather is carried out under the direct impulse of an individual idea.

Only with this view is true spiritual activity possible for the human being. If man does not bear *within himself* the grounds for his actions, but rather must conduct himself according to commandments, then he acts under compulsion, he stands under necessity, almost like a mere nature being.

Our philosophy is therefore pre-eminently a philosophy of spiritual activity.[9] First it shows theoretically how all forces, etc., that supposedly direct the world from outside must fall away; it then makes the human being into his own master in the very best sense of the word. When a person acts morally, this is not for us the fulfillment of duty but rather the manifestation of his completely free nature. The human being does not act because he ought, but rather be-

* *Ethical-spiritual Activity in Kant*, Mercury Press, 1987

cause he wants to. Goethe had this view in mind when he said: "Lessing, who resentfully felt many a limitation, has one of his characters say, 'No one has to have to.' A witty, jovial man said, 'Whoever wants to, has to.' A third, admittedly a cultivated person, added, *Whoever has insight, also wants to.'* " Thus there is no impetus for our actions other than our insight. Without any kind of compulsion entering in, the free human being acts in accordance with his insight, *in accordance with commandments that he gives himself.*

The well-known Kant-Schiller controversy revolved around these truths. Kant stood upon the standpoint of duty's commandments. He believed it a degradation of moral law to make it dependent upon human subjectivity. In his view man acts morally only when he renounces all subjective impulses in his actions and bends his neck solely to the majesty of duty. Schiller regarded this view as a degradation of human nature. Is human nature really so evil that it must completely push aside its own impulses in this way when it wants to be moral? The world view of Schiller and Goethe can only be in accord with the view we have put forward. The origin of man's actions is to be sought within *himself.*

Therefore in history, whose subject, after all, is man, one should not speak about outer influences upon his actions, about ideas that live in a certain time, etc., and least of all about a plan underlying history. History is nothing but the evolution of human actions, views, etc. "In all ages it is only individuals who have worked for science, not the age itself. It was the age that executed Socrates by poison; the age that burned Hus; *ages have always remained the same,*" says Goethe. All a priori constructing of plans that supposedly underlie history is in conflict with the *historical method* as it results from the nature of history. The goal of this method

112

is to become aware of what human beings have contributed to the progress of their race, to experience the goals a certain personality has set himself, the direction he has given to his age. History is to be based entirely upon man's nature. *Its* willing, *its* tendencies are to be understood. Our science of knowledge totally excludes the possibility of inserting into history a purpose such as, for example, that human beings are drawn up from a lower to a higher level of perfection, and so on. In the same way, to our view it seems erroneous to present historical events as a succession of causes and effects like facts of nature the way Herder does in his *Ideas for a Philosophy of the History of Mankind.* The laws of history are in fact of a much higher nature. A fact of physics is determined by another fact in such a way that the law stands *over* the phenomena. A historical fact, as something ideal, is determined by something ideal. There cause and effect, after all, can be spoken of only if one clings entirely to externals. Who could think that he is giving an accurate picture by calling Luther the cause of the Reformation? History is essentially a science of ideals. Its reality is, after all, ideas. Therefore devotion to the object is the only correct method. Any going beyond the object is unhistorical.

Psychology, ethnology, and history[10] are the major forms of the humanities. Their methods, as we have seen, are based upon the direct apprehension of ideal reality. The object of their study is the *idea*, the spiritual, just as the law of nature was the object of inorganic science, and the *typus* of organic science.

20. Optimism and Pessimism

The human being has proven to be the center of the world order. As spirit he attains the highest form of existence and in thinking carries out the most perfect process of the world. Only in the way he illuminates things are they real. This is a view from which it follows that the human being has within himself the basis, the goal, and the core of his existence. This view makes man into a self-sufficient being. He must find within himself the support for everything about himself. For his happiness also, therefore. If happiness is to be his, he can owe it to no one but himself. Any power that bestowed it upon him from outside would condemn him thereby to spiritual inactivity *(Unfreiheit)*. Nothing can give the human being satisfaction to which he has not first granted the ability to do so. If something is to cause us pleasure we ourselves must first grant it the power to do so. In the higher sense, pleasure and pain are there for the human being only insofar as he experiences them as such. With this, all optimism and all pessimism collapse. Optimism assumes that the world is such that everything in it is good, that it leads the human being into the greatest contentment. But if this is to be the case, he himself must first gain something that he wants from the world's objects; this means that he cannot become happy through the world but only through himself.

Pessimism, on the other hand, believes that the world is constituted in such a way that it leaves the human being eternally unsatisfied, that he can never be happy. The above objection is of course valid here also. The outer world in itself is neither good nor bad; it first becomes so through man. The human being would have to make himself unhappy if pessimism were to have any basis. He would have to carry within him the desire for unhappiness. But satisfying his desire would constitute precisely his happiness. To be consistent, the pessimist would have to assume that man sees his happiness in unhappiness. But then his view would after all dissolve into nothing. This one reflection shows clearly enough the erroneous nature of pessimism.

G. CONCLUSION

21. The Activity of Knowing and Artistic Creativity

Our epistemology has divested human knowing of the merely passive character often attributed to it and has grasped it as an *activity* of the human spirit. One usually believes that the content of science is taken up from outside; it is believed, in fact, that the more man's spirit refrains from any participation of its own in what is taken up, the more one will be able to maintain a high level of objectivity in science. Our considerations have shown that the true content of science is not at all the perceived outer material but rather the idea grasped in the spirit, which leads us deeper into the working of the world than all dissection and observation of the outer world as mere experience. The idea is the content of science. In contrast to perception, which is taken up passively, science is therefore a product of the activity of the human spirit.

With this we have brought knowing activity nearer to artistic creativity, which is also a productive, human activity. At the same time we have introduced the necessity of clarifying their mutual interrelationship.

Both knowing and artistic activity are based upon the fact that the human being lifts himself from reality as product to reality as producer; that he ascends from the created to the creating, from chance happening to necessity. Because outer reality always shows us only a creation of creative nature, we lift ourselves in spirit to the unity of nature that manifests to us as the creator. Each object of reality presents us with *one* of the endless possibilities lying hidden in the womb of creative nature. Our spirit lifts itself to the contemplation of that source in which *all* these possibilities are contained. Now science and art are the objects

117

into which the human being impresses what this contemplation offers him. In science this occurs only in the form of the idea, which means in a directly spiritual medium; in art it occurs in an object that is sense-perceptibly or spiritually *perceivable*. In science nature manifests in a purely ideal way as "that which encompasses everything individual"; in art an object of the outer world appears as *depicting* that which encompasses everything individual. That infinite element, which science seeks within the finite and seeks to present in the idea, is what art impresses into some medium taken from the real world. That which appears in science as idea is an image in art. The same infinite element is the object of both science and art, only it appears differently in one than in the other. The manner of presentation is different. Goethe therefore criticized the fact that one spoke of the idea of the beautiful as though the beautiful were not simply the sense-perceptible reflection of the idea.

Here we can see how the true artist must draw directly from the primal source of all existence, how he impresses into his works the necessity which, in science, we seek ideally in nature and spirit. Science seeks out the lawfulness in nature; art no less so, only it implants this lawfulness in addition into raw substance. A product of art is no less nature than a product of nature, only the lawfulness of nature has already been poured into the product of art in the way this lawfulness appeared to the human spirit. The great works of art that Goethe saw in Italy appeared to him as the direct copy of the necessity that man becomes aware of in nature. For him art is therefore also a manifestation of the secret laws of nature.

In a work of art everything depends upon the degree to which the artist has implanted the idea into his medium. The main thing is not *what* his subject is but rather *how* he handles it. If in science the externally perceived substance has to disappear completely so that only its essential being, the *idea*, remains, so in the product of art this substance has to remain—but the artistic treatment has to overcome completely anything about it of a particularized or chance nature. The object must be lifted entirely out of the sphere of chance and transferred into that of necessity. Nothing must remain in the artistically beautiful upon which the artist has not impressed *his* spirit. The *what* must be conquered by the *how*.

The overcoming of the sense-perceptible by the spirit is the goal of art and science. Science overcomes the sense-perceptible by dissolving it entirely into spirit; art does so by implanting spirit into the sense-perceptible. A statement of Goethe, which expresses these truths in a comprehensive way, may serve to bring our considerations to a close: "I think one could call science the knowledge of the general, abstracted knowledge; art, on the other hand, would be science turned into deed; science would be reason, and art its mechanism; therefore one could also call it practical science. And so, finally, science would be the theorem, art the problem."

Notes to the New Edition, 1924

1. Page 10:

"This literature . . . ": The attitude lying behind this assessment of the nature of philosophical literature and of the interest shown it arose out of the intellectual approach of scientific endeavor around the middle of the 1880's. Since then phenomena have come to light in the face of which this assessment no longer seems valid. One need think only of the brilliant insights that Nietzsche's thoughts and feelings have given into broad areas of life. And in the battles that took place and are taking place even today between materialistically thinking monists and the defenders of a spiritually oriented world view, there live both a striving of philosophical thinking for a life-filled content, and also a deep general interest in the riddles of existence. Paths of thought, such as those of Einstein springing from the world view of physics, have almost become the subject of universal conversation and literary expression.

But in spite of this the *motives* out of which this assessment was made back then are also still valid today. If one were to put this assessment into words today, one would have to formulate it differently. Since it appears again today almost as something ancient, it is quite appropriate to say how much this assessment is still valid.

Goethe's world view, the epistemology of which is to be sketched in this book, takes its start from what the *whole* human being experiences. With respect to this experience, *thinking* contemplation of the world is only *one* side. Out of the fullness of human existence thought-configurations rise, as it were, to the surface of soul life. One part of these thought-pictures constituted an answer to the question: What is the knowing activity of man? And this answer turns out to be such that one sees: Human existence reaches its potential only when it becomes active in knowing. Soul life without knowledge would be like a human organism without a head; i.e., it would not be at all. Within the inner life of the soul there grows a content which, just as the hungering organism demands nourishment, demands perception from outside; and, in the outer world, there is a content of perception which does not bear its essential being within itself, but which first reveals this essential being when the cognitive process connects this perceptual content with the soul content. In this way the cognitive process becomes a part in the formation of world reality. The human being works along creatively with this world reality through his knowing activity. And if a plant root is unthinkable without the fulfillment of its potential in the fruit, so by no means only man but the world itself would not be complete unless knowing activity took place. In his activity of knowing man does not do something for himself alone; rather he works along with the world in the revelation of real existence. What is in man is ideal semblance; what is in the world of perception is sense semblance; the interworking of the two in knowing activity first constitutes reality.

Seen in this way epistemology becomes a part of life. And it must be seen in this way when it is joined to the breadth of life of Goethean soul experience. But even Nietzsche's thinking and feeling do not connect themselves with this breadth of life. And still less so does that which otherwise has arisen as philosophically oriented views of life and of the world since the writing of what was characterized in this book as "The Point of Departure." All these views, after all, presuppose that reality is present somewhere outside of the activity of knowing, and that in the activity of knowing, a human, copied representation of this reality is to result, or perhaps cannot result. The fact that this reality cannot be *found* by knowing activity—because it is first made into reality in the activity of knowing—is experienced hardly anywhere. Those who think philosophically seek life and real existence outside of knowing activity; Goethe stands within creative life and real existence by engaging in the activity of knowing. Therefore even the more recent attempts at a world view stand outside the Goethean creation of ideas. *Our* epistemology wants to stand inside of it, because philosophy becomes a content of life thereby, and an interest in philosophy becomes necessary for life.

2. Page 11:

"The task of science is not to pose questions": Questions of knowing activity arise through the human soul organization in contemplation of the outer world. Within the soul impulse of the question there lies the power to press forward into the contemplation in such a way that this contemplation, together with the soul activity, brings the reality of what is contemplated to manifestation.

3. Page 20:

"This first activity of ours . . . can be called pure experience.": It is evident from the whole bearing of this epistemology that the point of its deliberations is to gain an answer to the question, What is knowledge? In order to attain this goal we looked, to begin with, at the world of sense perception on the one hand, and at penetration of it with thought, on the other. And it is shown that in the interpenetration of both, the true reality of sense existence reveals itself. With this the question, What is the activity of knowing? is answered in principle. This answer becomes no different when the question is extended to the contemplation of the spiritual. Therefore, what is said in this book about the nature of knowledge is valid also for the activity of knowing the spiritual worlds, to which my later books refer. The sense world, in its manifestation to human contemplation, is not reality. It attains its reality when connected with what reveals itself about the sense world in man when he thinks. Thoughts belong to the reality of what the senses behold; but the thought-element within sense existence does not bring itself to manifestation outside in sense existence but rather inside of man. Yet thought and sense perception are *one* existence. Inasmuch as the human being enters the world and views it with his senses, he excludes thought from reality; but thought then just appears in another place: inside the soul. The separation of perception and thought is of absolutely no significance for the objective world; this separation occurs only because man places himself into the midst of existence. Through this there arises for *him* the illusion that thought and sense perception are a duality. It is no different for spiritual contemplation. When this arises—through soul processes that I have described in my later book *Knowledge of the Higher Worlds and its Attainment*—it again constitutes only *one* side of spiritual existence; the corresponding thoughts of the spirit constitute the other side. A difference arises only insofar as sense perception completes itself, attains reality, through thoughts *upward*, in a certain way, to where the spiritual begins, whereas spiritual contemplation is experienced in its true being from this beginning point downward.* The fact that the experience of sense percep-

---

* Ein Unterschied tritt nur insofern auf, als die Sinneswahrnehmung durch den Gedanken gewissermassen *nach oben* zum Anfang des Geistigen hin in Wirklichkeit vollendet, die geistige Anschauung von diesem Anfang an nach unten hin in ihrer wahren Wesenheit erlebt wird.

tion occurs through the senses that nature has formed, whereas the experience of spiritual contemplation occurs through spiritual organs of perception that are first developed in a soul way, does not make a *principle* difference.

It is true to say that in none of my later books have I diverged from the idea of knowing activity that I developed in this one; rather I have only applied this idea to spiritual experience.

4. Page 21:

With respect to the essay "Nature": In my writings in connection with the "Goethe Society," I have tried to show that this essay has its origin in the fact that Tobler—who was in contact with Goethe in Weimar at the time this essay came into being—after conversations with Goethe, wrote down ideas that lived in Goethe as ones he recognized. What he wrote down then appeared in the *Tiefurt Journal*, which at that time was circulated only in a handwritten form. One finds in Goethe's writings a much later essay about this earlier publication. There Goethe states expressly that he does not remember whether the essay was his but that it contains ideas that were his at the time of its appearance. In my discussion in the writings of the "Goethe Society," I attempted to show that these ideas, in their further development, flowed into the whole Goethean view of nature. There have subsequently been published arguments claiming for Tobler the full rights of authorship for this essay "Nature." I do not wish to enter into the controversy on this question. Even if one credits Tobler with full originality in this essay, the fact still remains that these ideas did live in Goethe at the beginning of the 1780's and did so in such a way that—even according to his own admission—they prove to be the starting point of his comprehensive view of nature. Personally I have no reason to abandon my own view in this regard, which is that the ideas arose in Goethe. But even if they did not do so, they experienced in his spirit an existence that has become immeasurably fruitful. For the observer of the Goethean world view they are not of significance in themselves, but rather in relation to what has become of them.

5. Page 32:

"Manifestation to the senses": In this discussion there is already an allusion to the contemplation of the spiritual of which my later writings tell, in the sense of what is said in the above note to page 20.

6. Page 33:

"The situation would be entirely different . . . ": This discussion does not contradict contemplation of the spiritual; rather it points to the fact that for sense perception one can attain its essential being not, so to speak, by piercing the perception and penetrating to an existence behind it into its essential being, but rather by going back to the thought-element that manifests within man.

7. Page 83:

"Goethe's essay 'The Experiment as Mediator Between Subject and Object' ": It is interesting to know that Goethe wrote yet another essay in which he developed further his thoughts in the first essay about experimentation. We can reconstruct this second essay from Schiller's letter of January 19, 1798. There Goethe divides the methods of science into: *common empiricism*, which stays with the external phenomena given to the senses; *rationalism*, which builds up thought-systems upon insufficient observation, which, therefore, instead of grouping the facts in accordance with their nature, first figures out certain connections artificially, and then in fantastic ways reads something from them into the factual world; and finally *rational empiricism*, which does not stop short at common experience, but rather creates conditions under which experience reveals its essential being. [This note was to the first edition. To this, Rudolf Steiner added the further note in the second edition to the effect that the essay he "here assumed hypothetically, was actually discovered later in the Goethe-Schiller Archives and was included in the Weimar edition of Goethe's works."]

8. Page 96:

"This difference underlies . . . methods of inorganic science": One will find the "mystical approach" and "mysticism" spoken of in different ways in my writings. One can see in every case, from the context, that there is no contradiction among these different ways such as one has tried to fancy there. One can form a general concept of "mysticism." According to it, mysticism comprises what one can experience of the world through inner soul experience. This concept, first of all, cannot be disputed. For there is such an experience. And it reveals not only something about man's inner being but also something about the world. One must have eyes in which certain processes occur, in order to experience something about the realm of color. But through this one experiences not only something about the eye but also about the world. One must have an inner soul organ in order to experience certain things about the world.

But one must bring the full clarity of concepts into the experiences of the mystical organ if knowledge is to arise. There are people, however, who wish to take refuge in what is "inward" in order to flee the clarity of concepts. They call "mysticism" that which wants to lead knowledge out of the light of ideas into the darkness of the world of feeling— the world of feeling not illuminated by ideas. My writings everywhere speak *against* this mysticism; every page of my books, however, was written *for* the mysticism that holds fast to the clarity of ideas in thinking and that makes into a soul organ of perception that mystical sense which is active in the same region of man's being where otherwise dim feelings hold sway. This sense is for the spiritual completely like what the eye or ear is for the physical.

9. Page 111:

"Philosophy of spiritual activity *(Freiheit)*": The ideas of this philosophy have been developed further in my later *Philosophy of Spiritual Activity* (1894)*.

10. Page 113:

"Psychology, ethnology, and history are the major forms of the humanities": after having worked through the different areas of what I call "anthroposophy," I would now have to add anthroposophy to these were I writing this little book today. Forty years ago, as I was writing it, there stood before my mind's eye as "psychology"—in an unusual sense of the word, to be sure—something that included within itself the contemplation of the whole "spirit world" (pneumatology). But one should not infer from this that I wanted to exclude this "spirit world" from man's knowledge back then.

* *Philosophy of Spiritual Activity*, Anthroposophic Press, 1986